Leisure Painter

PROJECTS

J. McCombs 2000.

Leisure Painter

PROJECTS

TOP PROFESSIONAL ARTISTS REVEAL HOW TO PAINT A
WIDE RANGE OF POPULAR SUBJECTS USING ALL MEDIA

First published in 2002 by
Collins, an imprint of
HarperCollins*Publishers*
77-85 Fulham Palace Road
Hammersmith, London W6 8JB

The Collins website address is:
www.collins.co.uk

Collins is a registered trademark of HarperCollins Publishers Limited.

03 05 06 04 02
2   4   6   5   3   1

Editor: Diana Vowles
Designer: Caroline Hill

The text and illustrations in this book were previously published in
Leisure Painter Magazine.

ISBN 0 00 710773 0

Colour reproduction by Colourscan, Singapore
Printed and bound by Bath Press Colour Books

Page 1:
Lesley Hollands
China, Flowers and Lace
watercolour

Page 2:
John McCombs
Mother and Child
oil

Contents

Introduction

Leisure Painter's Painting Projects first appeared in the magazine in 1995 and quickly grew into one of its most popular series. Its aim was to provide readers with a practical exercise each month that they could work on at home – a form of home study that would be valuable not only to readers, but to tutors in their classrooms, who soon began to use Painting Projects as part of their study programmes.

Such was the popularity of the series that we decided to collaborate with HarperCollins on a book, which would make the projects and the expertise of our contributing authors available to a wider audience. The selection we bring you here, in media ranging from watercolour, oil, pastel and acrylic to line and wash and collage, represents the outcome – a feast of project treats to get you thinking as well as painting.

How the projects work

The idea behind the projects is simple. You are invited to study a photograph, or collection of photographs, provided by one of the 24 artists who have contributed projects to this book, and then to paint a picture based on it. In setting the project, the artist may point out elements within the photograph to look out for, such as aspects requiring special care or attention; he or she may offer some thoughts about format and

▼ **The Thames at Putney**
Ronald Morgan
Oil
23 × 30.5 cm
(9 × 12 in)

scale, the direction of the light source, or even which media to use. In some cases, the artist may set a specific task to address, such as working with a limited palette or changing the atmosphere of a scene. Preparatory sketches help to illustrate these first thoughts about the task in hand.

With this considered advice as a starting point, you are now invited to work on the set project yourself. The second part of each exercise reveals how the artist tackled the project and you will be able to compare your results. The artist explains his or her actions in full, taking the reader through each stage of the work from the very early planning right through to the finished painting, thereby giving an invaluable insight into the structure and techniques of his or her working practices.

Demonstrations and more

The value of the projects is two-fold. Not only do the readers receive a demonstration of how each of these artists works in their chosen media, but they are also given the opportunity to have a go themselves without any preconceptions of how to tackle the project before them. Essentially the projects get into the minds of the contributing artists, so that their thought processes are unravelled and the reasons for their tackling a scene in a particular way are revealed to us. Learning by these examples, the readers can begin to be more analytical in their approaches to

▲ **Ramparts, Hotel Palais Salaam, Taroudannt**
Christine McKechnie
Collage
44 × 46 cm
(17½ × 18 in)

painting and the results will be that much better for it.

The selection of 26 projects presented here will introduce you to the methods and media of some of *Leisure Painter*'s best-loved tutors; artists such as James Fletcher-Watson, Ann Blockley, David Curtis, Alwyn Crawshaw, Ray Campbell Smith and Wendy Jelbert. All of the artists featured are experts in their field and they have long been associated with the magazine, writing regular features on their working methods. In addition, since most of them are practising tutors as well, they are in touch with the needs of beginners and those relatively new to painting who are anxious to improve their techniques.

Themes and subjects

Popular subjects such as still life, landscapes, marinescapes and figure drawing are all

▶ **Hollyhocks**
Ann Blockley
Watercolour
30.5 × 20.5 cm
(12 × 8 in)

◀ **Gourds**
David Easton
Pastel on grey paper
30.5 × 30.5 cm
(12 × 12 in)

included, each one tackling that controversial problem of how to take a photograph as a starting point and use it in a creative and individual way – not creating a facsimile, but having the understanding and confidence to extract the elements that will create a well-balanced composition.

A number of the projects will stretch you still further with some thought-provoking exercises, such as Aggy Boshoff's fascinating exploration of multiple perspectives, using the work of David Hockney as inspiration; composite photographs combined with memory and imagination lead to a series of charming and telling pictures. Focusing on colour, Ronald Jesty invites readers to translate a dull, uninspiring photograph into a sun-filled painting using just the two complementary colours of yellow and purple.

In a similar vein, Stanford Gibbons encourages readers to understand ways of using the colour green by setting a project to paint a predominantly green scene without using the colour green anywhere at all in the work.

As readers work through this Painting Projects book, every single one of you will interpret a scene in a different way. Countless variables – of techniques, materials, cultures, skill, objectives or imagination – will conspire to produce works of total individuality. That is what makes painting such a challenging, personal and exciting journey. I hope it is one that you enjoy making.

Jane Stroud

Editor, *Leisure Painter*

Painting a landscape using just two colours

Ronald Jesty

Ronald Jesty sets the challenging task of translating greys into pure colours using tones of the complementary colours violet and yellow

Every so often I look through the pages of old sketchbooks to refresh my memory and derive ideas for subjects to paint. In doing this I rediscovered a pencil sketch of a dramatic-looking landscape in the north-west of Scotland. I had obviously been impressed by the rugged scenery and the sketch reminded me how fascinated I had been by the continuously changing patterns caused by the brilliant sunshine and the contrasting dark shadows of the swiftly moving clouds.

A photograph that I took at the time (*below*) shows a very grey scene – not what I remembered at all. Yet the notes on my sketch (*right*) also describe a series of violet-greys and yellow-greys, with a tonal range between 2 in the brightly lit areas and 6 to 7 in the dark shadows. These figures refer to a scale of 9 tones, 0 being white and 9 representing black. I find that it is most helpful when I am back in the studio to have precise descriptions of colours and accurate judgements of tone that can be relied upon.

Restrained palette

It occurred to me then that all these greys were in essence tints and tones of the complementary colours violet and yellow and that a painting might be made using only these colours – but in an exaggerated and emphatic way so as to create an exciting and colourful effect.

▲ *A photograph of the dramatic scenery in the far north-west of Scotland. Unfortunately the photograph did not succeed in capturing the exciting effects of brilliant sunshine and dark shadows on the landscape that so impressed the artist at the time.*

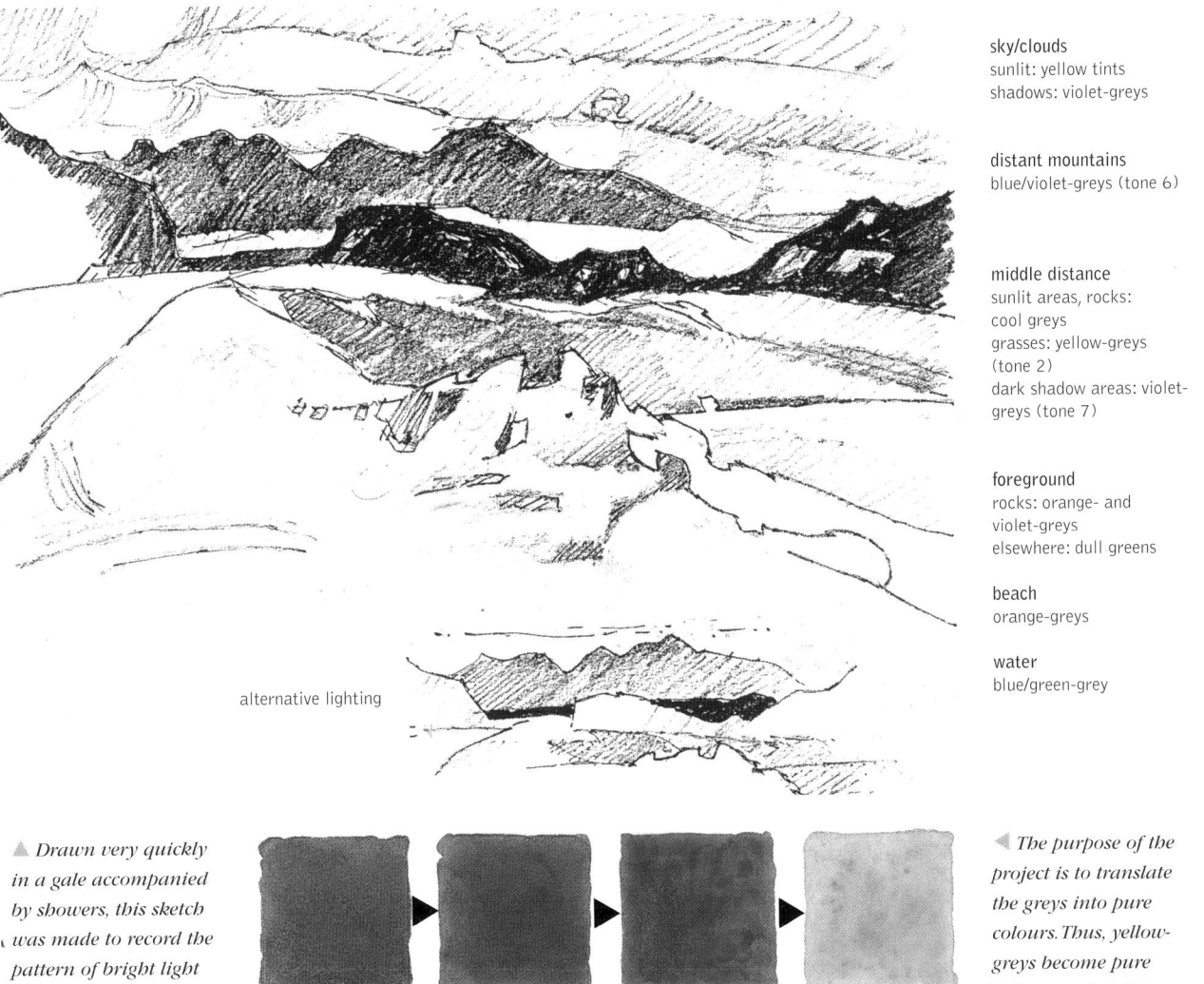

sky/clouds
sunlit: yellow tints
shadows: violet-greys

distant mountains
blue/violet-greys (tone 6)

middle distance
sunlit areas, rocks:
cool greys
grasses: yellow-greys
(tone 2)
dark shadow areas: violet-greys (tone 7)

foreground
rocks: orange- and
violet-greys
elsewhere: dull greens

beach
orange-greys

water
blue/green-grey

alternative lighting

▲ *Drawn very quickly in a gale accompanied by showers, this sketch was made to record the pattern of bright light and deep shadows on the landscape, together with colour notes. The smaller sketch below it shows another lighting effect.*

◀ *The purpose of the project is to translate the greys into pure colours. Thus, yellow-greys become pure yellows and violet-greys become pure violet in varying strengths.*

In order to achieve these more dramatic tints, violet-grey would be translated into a purer, more intense violet and yellow-grey would be pushed towards a fully saturated yellow, perhaps used straight from the tube of pigment without any dilution. In some passages it might be necessary, however, to darken a yellow – by means of adding its complementary colour, violet – which would have the opposite effect of reducing its relative brightness.

If you would like to try the kind of painting that I am suggesting but you feel unsure about the way the finished result will look, the best plan is to experiment initially by making a few preliminary colour sketches.

These need only be relatively small, as the purpose is merely to practise intensifying the complementary colours and seeing how they work against each other. Then, by referring to your own sketches and also using the information provided by my photograph and pencil drawing, you will have the means to work in a new, creative way, which you will find very exciting and satisfying.

Try to work in bright, pure colours as far as possible and keep the greys to a minimum. There will be many decisions to make as you study the various tones of grey and it will be necessary to keep the object of the project firmly in mind if you are to produce a painting with plenty of exciting colour.

11

The Method

Two examples of the complementary colours violet and yellow are shown opposite. In addition there are two neutrals, made by mixing the yellow and violet in different proportions, which are similar to some of the greys of the landscape that I noted on my sketch. Many variations of these mixtures could be made – more or less grey, paler, darker, more violet or yellow and so on. However, the purer (more saturated) hues are those I wanted to emphasize in this project.

Preliminary sketches

Since my chosen medium is watercolour where there is little scope for alteration, I wanted to gain a clear idea of how my painting would develop. To help me in this I made one or two small, quite rough, colour sketches in acrylic – a medium that allows adjustments and repainting. An example is shown here (*above*). Although unfinished and not definitive, it gave me an indication of the way things would go and what the finished work might look like. I always find these little preliminary experiments to be extremely useful in planning a painting and, importantly, an aid to one's confidence.

The colours I used in the painting were Lemon Yellow, Cadmium Yellow, Permanent Rose, Permanent Magenta, French Ultramarine and Coeruleum.

I first enlarged the sketch by means of a photocopy and traced the main outlines onto stretched Hot Pressed Arches watercolour paper. I continued by laying thin washes of the two yellows over the larger areas representing grass. A very weak mixture of Cadmium Yellow with a trace of Coeruleum was placed on the strip between the shapes of the two very dark hills and weak but pure Cadmium Yellow was washed into the lighter cloud areas.

I always like to begin a watercolour in this way, immediately covering as much of the white paper as possible. I now had some quite large areas tinted with yellows before adding the complementary violets to the shadows in the clouds and the darkly

silhouetted hills, which would then become the basis of the colour scheme. The violets were mixed from French Ultramarine and, variously, Permanent Magenta or Permanent Rose. In a few small places the blue and the magenta were used unmixed.

In watercolour, colours that are too bright can, if necessary, be made darker or more dull quite easily by overpainting. However, it is usually impossible to restore brightness to a dull colour. I was not too concerned, therefore, when my colours appeared to be rather vivid at this stage; after all, this was the reason for the exercise.

Sharper contrasts

By now, the pattern of contrasting yellows and violets was becoming apparent but, despite the constraints of the project, I needed to introduce what might be termed a 'darkened yellow' for the heavy shadow over the landscape behind the rocks in the centre of the picture. When I laid this dark, neutralized colour it had the desirable effect of giving added value to the surrounding brighter colours.

Finally, various smaller passages and a few details were painted in, using similar colour combinations and all the while seeking to

▲ *Preliminary sketches such as this help to clarify thoughts on colour and composition.*

A B C

▲ The colour patches referred to in the text. The greys in pair 'C' were made by means of adding yellow to violet and violet to yellow.

An infinite number of different greys and neutrals can be created by varying such mixtures of complementary colours.

◄ Detail of the finished watercolour.

▼ **Sutherland Landscape**
Watercolour
23 × 31 cm
(9 × 12¼ in)
Although essentially a violet/yellow colour scheme, red-violet and blue-violet have been used in various strengths in some places, such as the rocks on the left. The cooler Coeruleum blue has also been used to give colour variation – as in the water, foreground rocks and road. The dark shadow in the centre was made by adding violet to Cadmium Yellow until the required tone was reached.

place yellows adjacent to violets and warm colours against cool, such as in the pale rocks in the foreground.

This method of seeking out and using underlying colours is an excellent way of adding interest to what might otherwise be a rather dull subject. These underlying colours are always present in any scene, no matter what the subject may be, if only we look for them.

2

The Project
Studies in oil of figures outdoors

John McCombs

John McCombs shows how to translate a photograph with a limited colour range into a lively oil painting full of interest

A teacher friend of mine who is a keen photographer showed me some of his pictures of his holiday in the United States. Among them were some he had taken before his visit, of his pupils on an outdoor studies trip in Yorkshire. Although the American pictures were interesting and beautifully taken, from a painter's point of view I was more interested in the figurative photographs, and one in particular which really caught my eye with regard to composition, form and painterly possibilities.

My friend provided me with the negative, from which I had an 18 × 25.5 cm (7 × 10 in) print made. Not all of the figures in the photograph appealed to me, but the two young pupils sitting at the end of the park bench did because of the angularity of their postures and their concentration on their reading material. I cropped the photograph to include only the area that interested me and that is what is shown here. I hope you will find the subject interesting and will wish to paint it, but before you attempt to do so I would like to make some suggestions.

Directional quality

Composition should be the first consideration. No matter how well the picture is painted, if the composition is poor the work will never appear satisfactory. I think the height of the tall boy's head is well placed in the composition, but there should be more floor area below his boots in order to lift the arrangement and push the group back into the picture space.

Although the light is not strong, it does have a directional quality coming in from the left and it is important to keep this in mind when dealing with the light and shadowed areas.

The complex folds of the boy's clothing give a sculptural sense and it might be a good idea to think sculpturally when using the finer brush for drawing and cutting in, and when modelling the larger forms with the bigger brush.

There is no great range of colours in the subject, so you will have to make the most of the tall boy's red sweater complemented by the greens of the trees and bushes that constitute the background. The interest in the painting will mostly be in the forms and shapes, so employing some appropriate hard-edged line-work should give the subject a sharp delivery.

Space too has a shape, which is determined by the forms within it, so see it as a positive rather than a negative aspect of the work. Do not try to imitate texture. Keep the painting simple, direct and – above all – alive, even at the risk of it failing.

▲ *The photograph used as a starting point for the painting.*

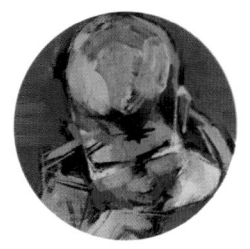

The Method

I have never been fond of oil painting on canvas, so I used to work on heavy but smooth watercolour paper. In recent years, I have preferred to work on the reverse side of mount card, which I find to be a more unyielding support that stands up well to rigorous brush and palette knife use. I do not size the card, but simply prime it with a liquid earth colour mix of Cadmium Orange (Hue) and Burnt Sienna. This prevents a too-rapid absorption of turpentine and oil into the card, while providing a colour base which, if evident at the finish of the painting, can give a colour-kick – especially against greens and other cool colours.

Another departure from tradition is that I do not like a hog hair brush for oil painting; I prefer to use a sable/synthetic blend instead. A No. 2 allows me to employ a fine brush line for drawing and the larger Nos. 4 and 5 are used for broader but controlled areas of colour.

Some years ago, my oil-painting technique gave rise to a thicker use of paint, which made working the picture difficult. Also, when varnished, the raised nodules of pigment reflected a displeasing shine, so I started using a knife to scrape away the unwanted mounds of colour. At the time I saw this as removing mistakes, but then I decided to use the scraping-down process as part of my technique.

Outdoor Studies was painted on card with sable/synthetic Sceptre Gold brushes Series 101 and was subjected to the knife.

Beginning the project

Two pieces of work came out of the project and I have described the first (*right*) as an oil sketch. I began by bonding the cropped photograph to a piece of offcut mount card so that I could stand it upright in front of me for easy reference, as the work throughout was to be based on a close observation of the subject. The sketch was started on a large piece of card with the intention of including the second figure, which at one point did

partially exist in the picture. This was eventually painted out and replaced by the bench when I realized that the painting, as a sketch, had reached what I felt was an interesting conclusion.

I started the painting with the small drawing brush, using rapid, energetic line. When I brought the larger brush into use I pushed and pulled the moderately thin paint across the surface, following the forms and emphasizing tension and movement. At such an early stage in the process I did not want to over-finish any one part but to develop the work through alteration and correction. The greenery in the background was just

▼ **Outdoor Studies**
Oil sketch
26 × 22 cm
(10¼ × 8¾ in)
In the preliminary oil sketch the composition was simplified and the treatment was understated.

▲ *Detail from the finished oil painting.*

how it appeared in the photograph. I kept the taller boy's head well up to the top of the picture, otherwise there would have been too much space that was absent of interest above the head of the smaller boy on the left. Also, I decided to leave out the third figure showing on the extreme left of the photograph, as I felt this detracted from the idea. Instead, as in the oil sketch, I replaced it with the shape of the bench. I allowed in more floor area to keep the taller boy's boots off the bottom of the painting, so pushing the group back into the picture space.

I tried to remain aware of the light, which, although weak, was directional. I emphasized this by strengthening the tone of the shadows on the ground.

My advice to readers was to imagine you were making a piece of sculpture when tackling this subject, and that is exactly what I did myself. I used the small brush for drawing and also for cutting and carving the shapes, and the larger brush for modelling the forms. This is more evident in the close-up detail showing the tall boy's head and hand (*left*).

I like to treat space in all subjects as a concrete reality, so here the brush was used in exploratory fashion for digging into, through and around the forms. I used the palette knife almost daily to prevent the paint from becoming too thick and doughy, hoping always that the scraping-down process might reveal some exciting undercolour to enliven the surface texture. As well as keeping my eye on the light, form and space within the subject, I tried to keep the brushwork lively and simply let the painting finish itself.

pushed in as patches of colour and, as with everything else, there was the intention of coming back to work on it further. However, tone, colour and texture suddenly seemed to come together in a lively finish, so I left it as it was.

After a minimum of scraping down with the knife I cropped the painting and amputated the feet, as the main areas of compositional interest in this sketch were the head, the hands and the book. The painting is very understated and the area around the book, if looked at in isolation from its surroundings, resembles a piece of abstract expressionism.

More floor area

I still wanted to make a painting showing the two figures, so I made a fresh start on the second version (*right*). Again I began with a small drawing brush, quickly sketching in the proportions.

My first concern on tackling the painting was to adapt the composition slightly from

▶ **Outdoor Studies**
Oil
40.5 × 30.5 cm
(16 × 12 in)
Strong forms and tones give the painting plenty of vitality in spite of the lack of a large range of colours. The main colour interest is in the red of the boys' clothing complemented by the green of the foliage behind them.

17

3

The Project

A cottage garden in the height of summer

Linda Birch

Linda Birch discusses ways of using mixed media and takes a new approach to a traditional cottage-garden scene

We did a deal, Mrs Potter and I. She taught me how to make bread and I painted her garden. Some money did change hands, but I now make the best bread ever, and I got tremendous pleasure out of painting the garden. These photographs and sketches were done between the proving of the bread on one of those summer days I remember as being idyllically sunny and warm.

The Potters live in a house that was built on a medieval strip – hence the long, slim shape of the garden. It is laid out to flowers, herbs, vegetables and a small grassed area with fruit trees. The area is bounded by dry-stone walls of Pennine sandstone. I include two slightly different views.

The first view

What attracted me about this picture (*below*) was the strong shape made by the buildings at the back. The yard is partly in the light and the sun on the house roof indicates the warmth and sunshine of a July day. The soft shadow on the stone walls contributes luminous greys.

Notice the curve of the path, together with the shadow on the left across the garden. This corresponds to the zigzag shape of the larger house. I felt that the two windows facing outwards could be a focal point, but they were not quite strong enough to hold the eye. Whenever you paint or draw, it is important to keep in mind that what you do is a statement. It says: 'Look at this – I find this interesting.' It is not merely a record of what is there. Here I considered that the eye needed something other than the windows to use as a focal point – a figure, perhaps.

The second view

The other view of the garden (*top right*) shows the flowers in the foreground. It is a looser, more sprawling composition than the first, but I wanted to include the delphiniums and daisies in my painting because of their luminosity in shadows.

▲ *View 1, photographed at approximately 11.30 a.m. on a mid-July day when the weather was warm and sunny.*

▶ *A tiny plan drawing made with a pencil helps to establish the main shapes of the composition.*

In your own painting you are at liberty to add or subtract flowers as you like. You can mix the two compositions if you wish, and use portrait (upright) or landscape format.

Some possibilities

The use of mixed media is sometimes viewed with suspicion by purists, but I maintain that any means justifies the end. You control the painting because it is a vehicle for what you want to say. Here are some possibilities of mixed media for you to think about:

Line and wash Pen or pencil with a watercolour wash added.

Wash and line Watercolour washes, defined and enhanced with pen or pencil line.

Watercolour and coloured pencil Washes with coloured pencil added when dry. This is particularly good for texture.

Watercolour and tissue (collage) A base of watercolour is laid. When it is dry, glue is applied then white tissue paper is stuck over the surface. Watercolour is repainted on top.

Coloured inks and tissue As above, with a watercolour base and inks on top.

Watercolour and pastel A watercolour base, with pastel used on top when it is dry.

Watercolour and charcoal The painting is done in watercolour. When it is dry, charcoal is rubbed over the surface to cover the picture. Light parts are lifted out with a putty eraser.

Watercolour and Conté crayon This is best used monochromatically. Light washes of one colour are applied, working from light to near dark. Black or dark brown crayon is used for darks, texture and form.

Oil pastels and watercolour Because oils and water do not mix, this is an interesting combination. The oil pastel is used over or under the watercolour for textural passages.

 *View showing the flower garden. The prominent flowers are delphiniums, larkspur, Canterbury bells and white daisies.*

It is important to make a tonal scheme as this can affect the success of the painting considerably.

The Method

Oil pastel and watercolour, with the oil pastel laid first.

I decided to use mixed media – coloured inks and tissue paper – to do a collage. There was a lot of texture, particularly in the foreground, and the wrinkling quality of tissue when wet would render some of the effects I wanted. The luminous blues of the flowers in the foreground could be exploited using transparent inks. The richness of colour together with the accidental properties that tissue has (you never quite know what will happen) would be interesting to explore.

The materials I used were: white tissue paper; a glue stick (any PVA-type glue will work); Magicolor Liquid Acrylics, which are transparent and resemble coloured inks; a piece of white card, for which watercolour paper or stretched cartridge paper could be substituted; watercolour paints; some watercolour brushes – old ones, as acrylic colour and inks can damage them if they are allowed to dry; and an old palette.

I decided to work with the second view but to crop it into a portrait format. This would include the pale flowers in the foreground and part of the building next door on the right. I liked the shape of the rooftops, which acted as an anchor and a foil for the loose and rounded plant shapes in the front. Using my artistic licence to move objects around in the picture, I revealed the window on the right by cutting down the plant climbing the wall.

I also felt there ought to be signs of life in the painting, but that a figure would crowd the composition. I settled for a washing line instead, thereby introducing a minimal sign of human activity.

First I drew out the composition, merely placing things in their right positions rather than doing a detailed drawing. Next, I laid in a series of washed colours that approximated to a pale version of the colours I eventually wanted. This would help me to see where I was going once the tissue was in place. It is important at this stage not to apply too much colour. Indeed, sometimes I do not lay any at all if the drawing shows clearly under the tissue. Inks rely on the whiteness of the paper to render the transparency of their colour, and too much underpainting will prevent this.

I then tore the tissue paper into small pieces, ranging from matchbox size to bits about 4 cm (1½ in) across. You can lay a whole sheet of tissue, although the random wrinkling will not be as varied. Do not cut the pieces, as torn edges assist the textural qualities of the collage.

When the initial colour washes were dry, it was time to stick the tissue in place. Cover the whole surface with tissue – it does not matter if the pieces overlap slightly. Any pieces that do not fully adhere to the surface usually stick when the ink goes on, or you can apply more glue.

Adding the next layer

The Magicolors I used in my painting were Royal Blue, Process Blue, Process Yellow, Flesh, Mars Red, Grecian Olive, Golden Sand and Earth Brown. It is best to work from light to dark, so the sky and light parts of the greenery and flowers were applied first. At this stage you can place the light colour all over the object and succeeding darker tones can be built up over the top.

Do not panic when you first put the colour on. The tissue will immediately wrinkle and the ink will seep under the paper, giving an

◄ The early stage, showing the initial drawing with a pale watercolour wash. Tissue was then glued over the surface. Note the creeping of the ink under the tissue surface, which gives the rich batik-like effect. This makes it ideal for textured surfaces.

▼ Mrs Potter's Garden
Inks and tissue
30.5 × 24 cm
(12 × 9½ in)
The surface can be varnished to seal it, although it would be better mounted and framed under glass.

appearance resembling batik. If you are not accustomed to the inks, try mixing them with a little water to pale them slightly for the first coat of colour. You can then build up the colour gradually.

Before finishing I used a nibbed pen with brown ink to pick out detail. Finally, I glazed a mix of Process Yellow and Golden Sand with a little water over the whole surface (including the blue flowers) to enrich it further. This is also a good way to pull any disparate colours together. When the painting is finished it can be varnished to seal it, but as the surface is rather fragile it is better to frame it under glass.

If you are painting a strongly coloured subject, try using coloured tissue with inks. A Byzantine richness of colour can be achieved. With richly coloured large flowers, such as rhododendrons or peonies, this technique is superb. Tear your paper to match the motif you are covering, using larger, flatter shapes for skies, for example, and smaller rounded shapes for flowers.

An unpredictable path

You may well feel that mastering watercolour or any other single medium is quite enough to take on without complicating matters. However, there are good reasons for exploring the use of available media a little further. There is in all of us a desire to have some control over what we are doing; to know what the end result will be. We want to succeed at what we do; failure is something to be avoided. So we take a safe option and stick with the familiar.

Yet we are not in control at all. We merely tread a well-known path each time. 'This is how we lay a wash to get a certain result.' 'Put the trees here, and the picture will work better.' 'Do that, and this will happen.' However, following a prescribed route to a desired end is predictable and eventually dull. There is no creativity this way.

Sometimes it is good to try things you have not done before. Treat the endeavour as an exercise. That way you will be less bothered about making mistakes, and more relaxed about the business of exploring a new technique or medium. You will find that your attitude to your paintings will be revitalized, and it is even said that our brains become more active and fertile the more we concern ourselves with creative things. Not only that, the ageing process is less marked – so it must be worth experimenting with your painting!

4

The Project
The River Orwell in pastel

Margaret Glass

Margaret Glass shows the power of the artist, adapting the photograph to suit her purposes

For most of my life I have lived near to the east coast and so marine subjects are my first love. The photograph of the River Orwell at Pin Mill in Suffolk (*below*) was taken one clear sunny afternoon. It is quite a complex subject and some simplification will be needed to avoid the picture becoming too busy. The overall colour scheme is very blue, with the reflection of sky in water, and I feel that some thought needs to go into this; the importance of achieving aerial perspective with the use of warm and cool colours should be kept in the forefront when selecting your palette.

Balancing the picture

The composition of the photograph needs some alteration. First, the space between the distant barge and the foreground boat is too great; the eye tends to jump from one side of the picture to the other. My solution was to move the barge over to the left of centre, with the foreground grasses and the wooden posts, the barge and the foreground boat creating a circle of interest. I felt that the clouds needed more space, so I planned to add some blue sky at the top. This was all very roughly worked out in my first sketch (*bottom*).

The foreground clutter needed to be simplified and I also decided it would create more atmosphere if I placed warmer colours in the clouds, changing the time of day to later in the afternoon. Such is the power we artists can wield! These colours would be reflected in the water and would add interest to detract from the foreground clutter. This would also get around the problem of the painting being too blue.

Transferring to glass paper

My basic compositional sketch was quickly drawn in on glass paper that I had previously mounted onto MDF board. The size was 30.5 × 40.5 cm (12 × 16 in), which is fairly small for a large scene, but this would keep under control the detail that I might otherwise have gone for. I wanted to convey the day, the feel of this high tide lapping onto the shore and the reflections on the rippling water. The boats are incidentals; they may make the composition but they are not the whole story.

▲ *The River Orwell at Pin Mill in Suffolk is the subject of this project in pastel.*

◄ *Margaret's basic sketch to establish the composition.*

The Method

Having simplified and rearranged the composition to give a more pleasing picture and also altered the time of day to bring warmer colours to the palette, I was now ready to embark upon my painting of this peaceful scene of boats on a Suffolk river. I had decided to use very soft pastels and glass paper in order to achieve a painterly effect that I felt would be particularly appropriate for the subject.

I started with a dark blue-grey pastel, using it to put in the horizon line and tree line as well as the dark tones of the boats, sky and clouds. A suggestion of green was applied to the distant trees that rise behind the water and warm yellow was introduced in both water and sky (*above*).

Working on the sky

It was important to base the colour of the sky on the strong dark of the horizon line and, although the initial cool blue was very strong, it would calm down when covered with a warm blue of a similar tone. As the sky and its reflection are the main elements of the painting, I worked upon them next.

I placed the darkest and therefore the strongest colours in first. These were then

▲ *In the early stages the horizon and tree lines were established as well as the dark tones of the boats.*

▶ *The reflections of the sky were added to the water, repeating the same colours as those used in the sky.*

▼ *Detail of the sky, showing the range of tones.*

▶ *The strong colours of the boats also appeared in the reflections here and there.*

▼ *The detail in the foreground boat makes it convincingly solid.*

controlled by placing the middle tones alongside and on top, before finally adding the highlights. The sky above the clouds was a mixture of warm and cool blue, paling down to the horizon with a cool blue and green to achieve a sense of recession. The reflections of the sky were also placed in the water at this stage, using exactly the same colours as those used in the sky.

Building layers

The next stage of the work was to paint the background trees and the brightly coloured boats in the middle ground. I employed a slightly different technique to that used in the sky, putting only one layer of pastel on my paper. When one layer is placed on top of another, it sinks into that first colour and is therefore diluted. Since I wanted the brilliance of colours that depict late sunlight,

the first stroke of pastel would be the brightest I could achieve.

For the background trees and fields, I worked a strong orange with a blue-grey and added highlights of warm green and yellow. I introduced this same orange into the masts and superstructure of the boats in order to help create a unity of colour throughout the picture. I worked from dark to light, selecting the correct tonal values and the brightest colours that I dared.

Next I put in more detail on the boats in the middle distance and the foreground fishing boat. I deliberately kept the masts and metal framework of these boats fairly high key so that they would not draw unnecessary attention. My intention was that there should be enough detail to achieve the illusion of solid boats, rather than giving the viewer a faithful lesson on rigging.

The reflections of the boats were put in using the same colours. When painting water, it is vital that the strokes of pastel are kept absolutely horizontal. Even with waves breaking the surface, water is the flattest thing you can paint in nature.

The final touches

Reaching the end of the painting, I put in a few strokes of green in order to suggest the foreground reeds. The reflection of the masts and posts happily join the foreground to the middle ground and the masts link to the sky. The finished work achieves, for me, the atmosphere of a really beautiful day at Pin Mill with the promise of a warm, still evening to come.

▲ **The River Orwell at Pin Mill**
Pastel
30.5 × 40.5 cm
(12 × 16 in)
Warm colours and blue sky evoke the feeling of late afternoon on a sunny summer day.

5

The Project
Painting at home from past memories

Alwyn Crawshaw

Alwyn Crawshaw selects images of Japan, collected on his travels and painted back home in his studio

No matter how long we have been painting, we artists get excited when we see a subject that inspires us. We want to paint it there and then but, unfortunately, life does not work like that. One of the most frustrating times is when we are on a car journey and cannot stop. The views we see slip past and are gone. The images can stay with us in our visual memory and the only way to paint them then is at home. If we are lucky and there is a chance to photograph the scenes, we have something to help our memory.

Perhaps the most frustrating time is when we are in a new location, either for a holiday or just a day trip. We get excited, drinking in the atmosphere and visual images as we travel around, sketching (if there is time) and taking photographs. When we return home, with the wealth of information that we have – sketches, photographs and visual memory – the decision of what to paint can become confusing. This is because we remember the place through a haze of many images that seem to materialize in one glorious, unpaintable scene. How do we sort things out? Let me explain how I solved this problem when I went to Japan with my wife June for our exhibition in Tokyo.

▲ *Pencil sketches of bicycles.*

Deciding the subject

In Tokyo I did some sketches, absorbed the atmosphere and took photographs. I was excited most by the bustling and very colourful street scenes. I had done some sketches of street scenes in watercolour and pencil and decided that one in particular (*left*) would be what I would paint first. I also had a photograph of the scene. However, when I looked at the sketch and photograph, the image did not come up to the one in my visual memory (the one with the whole of Tokyo in one scene). I started to search further through my sketchbook and photographs.

We had rain during our stay and I looked at photographs with shiny reflections on the streets and dozens of raised umbrellas. I was also inspired by the number of bicycles. I had done some quick pencil sketches of bicycles (*above*) and umbrellas. The weather at times had been very hot and this left a strong impression, so all the information was there, both visual and emotional. The problem, though, was to choose what to paint.

Eventually, I decided to work from a photograph (*above right*), not my sketch. This was because the photograph of the sketch scene was not very good and I felt there was not enough detail in the sketch alone to make

▼ *A sketch of a street scene in Tokyo.*

a larger painting. The photograph I had chosen also had bicycles.

The next decision was the atmosphere to create. I did a preliminary sketch on paper with a 2B pencil and watercolour to experiment with the rain, reflections and umbrellas (*below*). However, although I love the shiny surfaces and reflections of a rainy painting, I eventually decided on a hot sunny day because the heat of some of those streets had left a lasting impression on me.

So, after a morning of decisions and counter-decisions I had decided what to paint. I had also built up my enthusiasm and got all my inspiration back.

▲ *Eventually Alwyn decided to work from this photograph.*

The project

I decided to paint with Daler-Rowney's Cryla Flow acrylics because I felt they were right for the time and for the subject. I used Cryla sketching paper, which is a very good quality paper made especially for Cryla painting. It needs no priming and is ready to use. I worked with Daler-Rowney Cryla brushes, Series C25, and a sable, Series 43, No. 6.

Work from my photograph, but use your creativity to alter the composition, colouring or atmosphere as you want. When you are working from your own holiday sketches and photographs, remember these tips:

1 If there is not much time, sketch in pencil. The fact of seeing (observing) and drawing, no matter how simple, will give you valuable general knowledge of the subject to work on at home.

2 If you have a sketch and a photograph of the scene, use the sketch as your main starting point and the photograph for factual and detail features.

3 Take time to look through your photographs and sketches. This will bring back memories and build up your enthusiasm, inspiring you to paint.

4 Fix your mind on a particular atmosphere and stick to it as you paint. Do not let your mind wander off on to other types of days.

▶ *A preliminary sketch of a rainy subject.*

The Method

Before picking up a pencil or paint brush I spent some time looking at my photograph and sketches – and thinking. The most important question: was there anything that worried me about the photograph? The first thing that concerned me was the white van. I decided it did not help the painting, so I took it out. The area behind the van was simple to re-create. I just continued the shop front and put in some people.

The photograph was very contrasty, with strong darks and lights. However, I remembered the scene being more soft and hazy, and this is the way I painted it. More importantly, as well as being very warm it was very humid, and I felt that the crisp sunlight in the photograph did not convey that.

▲ *The street scene was first blocked in with a watercolour technique.*

The overall colouring of the photograph was a little cold, so I warmed all the colours up in my painting. The strong, angular shadows on the road in the foreground were too dominant, so I gave them irregular shapes. Although shadows cast from buildings are inevitably square and angular, mine could be shadows cast from flags or decoration on the building. Finally, if the lettering on the shop's banners reads something it should not, my defence is that I do not speak Japanese and I used my artist's licence.

Light to dark

I started the picture by drawing in the main features with an HB pencil, ignoring detail. I worked the painting in three stages. First I blocked in the whole of the painting in a watercolour technique (*left*). Thicker opaque paint was then used and the third stage was refining and adding any detail.

In the first stage I did not use any white paint. I mixed plenty of water with the paint and kept the colours cool and soft in the background and stronger and warmer in the foreground. Because the colours are transparent at this stage, work from light to dark as you progress. If something happens in the watercolour technique that you do not like, remember that you will be going over the work in places with opaque paint, so you can correct areas where necessary.

When you use the paint thicker and opaquely, do not put much work into the background. Keep it simple to give the impression of distance. I put more opaque paint work on the shadow areas, making them darker, and added a little more modelling to them. I then painted in some detail. The figures were worked on, then the shops on the right and the lettering on the banners. Finally, I added some more darks and lights where I felt they were needed.

I hope you enjoyed the project. Now get out your own sketches and photographs and enjoy a trip down memory lane. I am sure that the journey will build up your enthusiasm.

French Ultramarine

Crimson

Cadmium Yellow

Raw Sienna

Cadmium Red

Bright Green

Coeruleum

Raw Umber

Titanium White

▲ *The acrylic Cryla Flow colours that were used for the painting*

▲ **Tokyo Street Scene** (18 × 14 in)
Acrylic
45 × 35.5 cm

Alwyn's depiction of a street scene in Tokyo.

6

A landscape in watercolour

Ray Campbell Smith

Ray Campbell Smith looks at ways to overcome the shortcomings of photographs in order to create successful watercolours

The south-eastern corner of England is now one of the most built-up areas of the country, but you can still find plenty of traditional Kentish farms with their warm bricks made from Wealden clays and their conical oasthouses topped by white-painted cowls.

The farmhouse scene in the photograph shown below is an attractive one, but it does present the artist with a number of problems that can be resolved by altering it here and there to improve the composition. Unless you have been commissioned to paint a particular subject, when you can hardly take liberties with the local topography, the demands of producing a pleasing and well-balanced composition must take precedence over verisimilitude.

Improving the composition

Perhaps the most pressing problem is the hard, almost horizontal line separating the foreground stubble field from the expanse of buildings and foliage beyond. This needs to be broken or softened. The horizon is too close to the halfway mark, but this can easily be resolved by moving it up or down. The colour, too, needs careful consideration: the red of the tiles and bricks looks a bit persistent and you should look for other, more subtle colours and make the most of them.

There is not much colour variety in the foliage of the trees and bushes either and here again it will pay to look for any variations you can identify and perhaps exaggerate them a little. The white oast cowls hardly register against the pale sky, so you should look for some way of increasing the tonal contrast. You will think of further ways to effect improvement, so give your imagination full rein and remember you are not just copying a photograph, but are using the information it contains to produce an attractive painting of your own.

▲ *The farm buildings that are so typical of the Kentish landscape.*

▶ *It is always useful to make a preliminary tone sketch to help sort out lights and darks. Ray has made no attempt here to improve the composition.*

The Method

◀ *Ray's monochrome sketch in watercolour of the amended composition.*

I began by making a quick monochrome sketch in watercolour to establish my ideas for improving the composition (*above*). My solution to the problem of the strong, unbroken horizontal separating the foreground stubble from the scene above it was to introduce a farm track running diagonally into the cluster of farm buildings, which effectively broke this hard line and also provided some much-needed variety in the foreground. It had the added advantage of leading the viewer's eye into the heart of the painting.

The proximity of the horizon to the half-way mark was dealt with by the simple expedient of lowering the horizon. I could of course have raised it, but as the sky was quite a lively one and the stubble foreground lacked interest, lowering the horizon seemed the better option. I decided to make much more of the line of distant blue-grey hills and, as you can see, they feature far more tellingly in the painting than they do in the photograph, their cool tones making a pleasing chromatic contrast with the warm colours of the farm buildings.

You may notice that I have slightly altered the angle of the farmhouse on the right of the painting. If you look at the photograph you will see that the dormer windows appear to be looking straight out of the picture, carrying the eye of the viewer with them, a fault which the altered angle corrects by eliminating them from the picture altogether.

Adding variety

The trees in the photograph are all of similar height, so I made a conscious effort to vary their size – a change that adds interest to their composition. The large tree on the left also acts as a 'stop' and keeps the eye in the painting. I planned my sky so that there would be an area of cloud shadow behind the oast houses – a ploy that enables their white cowls to register more effectively. At the same time I simplified the cloud formations so that the softer, smoother treatment would contrast better with the busy scene below and not compete with it.

The foreground shadow seen in the photograph, cast by a tree situated out of the picture, helped to break up the expanse of foreground stubble and here I went one better and introduced a second, rather larger, shadow.

The colours in the photograph are not as subtle as I remember them on the ground: the reds of the buildings and the greens of the foliage are a little hard and lacking in variety. I therefore looked for colour variation

▲ *Detail of the finished painting, showing the wet-into-wet washes in the sky.*

wherever I could and you will see hints of green on the lower courses of the tiled roofs and some warmer tones in some of the trees and hedges.

So much for the changes I considered necessary. I wonder if yours are along similar lines or whether you have found entirely different solutions.

Getting started

When I was satisfied with my sketch, I drew in the main features with a 2B pencil on my watercolour paper, which was Arches 140 gsm (300 lb) Rough.

If you are not sufficiently confident to draw directly on your support, always make a sketch of similar size first and transfer this, if necessary by tracing, onto your paper. Alterations made on your watercolour paper can do considerable harm and jeopardize the purity and clarity of subsequent washes. I do

no more drawing than is absolutely essential and never outline trees or bushes, preferring to describe their complex forms by means of lively brushwork. Where subtle perspectives are involved some careful drawing is, however, necessary.

The painting process

Now for the painting. I began by masking the oasthouse cowls, as it would have been tricky to paint round their precise shapes while applying full liquid washes to the sky. These washes were three in number: a pale one of Raw Sienna for the lower sky and, further diluted, for the sunlit clouds; a mixture of French Ultramarine and Light Red for the cloud shadows; and a blend of French Ultramarine and Winsor Blue for the upper sky. I allowed these washes to merge together but preserved a few hard-edged highlights here and there. The cloud shadows were largely horizontal, decreasing in strength and depth as they approached the horizon, to suggest the perspective of the receding cloud formations.

Shadows play an important part in painting buildings and help to give them a three-dimensional appearance. It is worth waiting until the sun is in the optimum position to produce the most effective shadows, as I did when taking the photograph.

For the warm-coloured tiles and brickwork of the farm buildings I used various blends of Raw Sienna, Burnt Sienna, Light Red and Burnt Umber, with touches of green (Raw Sienna with a little Winsor Blue) to suggest moss and algae. The shadows were mainly French Ultramarine and Light Red, with the addition of Burnt Sienna to indicate reflected light. I left the weatherboarding of the centre barn white as I felt this would provide a crisper note than the brown that can be seen in the photograph. I also increased the size of this barn so that it would contribute more to the composition.

The two taller trees went in next and for these I used Raw Sienna, a touch of Burnt Sienna and Payne's Grey, with a stronger mix of the last two for the shadowed area and the branches. Only then did I paint the blue-grey distant ridge, using a mixture of French Ultramarine and Light Red, adding a touch of Raw Sienna lower down where decreasing distance would lessen the greying effect.

When these washes were dry I added an impression of distant woods and hedges in French Ultramarine and Light Red. Most

painters tackle the distant scene before the foreground and leave unpainted areas for the buildings and trees. This is fine for the straight lines of the buildings, but less satisfactory for the outlines of the trees. Painting the trees first enables one to employ free brushwork to capture the broken outlines. It is then a simple matter to apply the wash for the distant hills right up to the outlines of the buildings and foliage.

Finishing touches

I painted the hedgerows very loosely, varying both height and colour as I did so. The colours were various blends of Raw Sienna, Burnt Sienna and Winsor Blue, plus Payne's Grey for the shadows. The sandy-coloured farm track was pale Raw Sienna with some soft horizontal shading in French Ultramarine and Light Red. This left just the foreground stubble, which presented something of a

problem, as any attempt to paint individual stalks would have led to over-complication and over-working. I finally decided upon a broken wash of dilute Raw Sienna with a touch of Burnt Sienna and, when that was dry, I added the tree shadows in French Ultramarine and Light Red, allowing the roughness of the paper to play its part in producing broken outlines. This completed the watercolour – a creative adaptation of the photograph that was its starting point.

▲ **Kentish Farm Buildings**
Watercolour
28 × 39 cm
(11 × 15¼ in)
Unmistakably a Kentish scene – but one altered subtly from reality to make a more pleasing composition.

The Project
7

A Cotswold scene using pen and wash

Michael Edwards

Michael Edwards sets the scene for an unusual technique involving watercolour and water-soluble ink

Light rain made painting or sketching impossible at the time I saw this attractive scene in the Cotswolds, so I took a photograph instead. The result was uninspiring – certainly not the sort of picture that makes you rush to your paints. But, before you discard a photograph like this, take a closer look to see whether you can rescue the scene and still make a pleasing picture from it.

The composition is poor – the house is too far to the right and the barn is separated from it, making two centres of interest. The front of the house is obscured by trees and bushes. There is no light to give the picture life or the buildings a three-dimensional form. So, what could be done?

First I made a quick pencil sketch on a piece of scrap paper, adjusting the composition by moving the house more towards the centre and putting the barn closer to the house. This makes a principal focus on the house and a secondary focus on the barn.

I placed extra trees to the right of the house and a bush in the foreground left, making the lane a more definite route into the picture. From this rough sketch I could see that the composition could be improved sufficiently to make a reasonable painting.

Next I added details to the front of the house, using artistic licence to include windows and doors that did not appear in the photograph, and eliminated several other bushes that did not benefit the sketch.

Turning on the sun

I realized that if the sun were shining from the right the front of the house would be in full sunlight, adding a strong central point of interest, and clouds in the sky could be used to help the composition. Also, the trees on the right would throw shadows across the drive, creating light and shade in the foreground. The sketch now had all the elements needed to create an interesting, lively painting.

▲ *Michael's photograph of the Cotswold farmhouse and barn.*

▶ *This exploratory sketch improves the composition. Michael has moved the house more to the centre, made the barn closer to the house and eliminated the bushes and trees in front of the house. The details of windows and front door were made up. Extra trees have been added to the right and a bush inserted to the left.*

The Method

◄ A simplified drawing was used, as detail would be added later in pen. The initial washes were applied with the concentration on colour and tone and keeping the washes clean.

The medium I decided to employ was pen and wash, but with a significant difference from most pen and wash paintings as I prefer water-soluble ink, which is used chiefly for calligraphy. It is permanent and is available in various colours, though I use mainly black and brown. As it is water-soluble I have to put the ink on top of the watercolour, whereas most pen and wash paintings use waterproof Indian ink, which is applied first. By using a water-soluble ink, I can apply water to some of the ink passages to create special effects.

Different watercolour papers have dramatically varying impacts on the way a painting can be tackled. Not only does the texture of the paper result in different effects, with Not, Rough, and Hot Pressed all reacting individually to the brush, but the chemical composition of the paper also affects the way that watercolour can be manipulated. It is valuable for any watercolour painter to try various papers to discover their impact on painting techniques. The paper used in this painting was 140 gsm (300 lb) Saunders Waterford with a Not finish.

Beginning the painting

First I drew the outline of the painting, using a 2B pencil. I did not put in details such as windows, branches and twigs as I knew that I would be adding these in ink later.

I then painted a preliminary watercolour wash concentrating on tones and colours, but not including shadows and leaving the sky blank (*above*). I used colours to suggest autumn – Vandyke Brown (Hue), Burnt Sienna and Yellow Ochre. The light on the grass in the foreground was Lemon Yellow, with Coeruleum to create the cooler tones in the foreground. I kept the washes clean, wherever possible using a single wash as I prefer to change colours and tones wet-in-wet rather than add another wash on top. At this early stage the painting looked quite flat and simple.

Next I washed on the sky, using a large No. 24 Pro Arte 101 brush. Using Coeruleum

▶ *With the sky and shadows added, the tonal balance was improved. Note how the clouds and shadows also contribute to the composition.*

with a touch of Alizarin Crimson, I added broad washes, leaving the paper white in areas to indicate clouds. I then coloured these with Naples Yellow. On the right-hand side of the painting, I washed the Coeruleum down the side of the paper to the bottom in order to fade out the edge of the picture. I also added some shadows of a similar colour (Coeruleum and French Ultramarine) across the barn, behind the house, across the foreground along the edge of the drive and

from the trees, across the grass and drive. These shadows, which were put in rapidly, suddenly brought the picture much more into focus (*above*).

The benefit of adding the sky at this stage is that you can adjust the tone, colour and shape of the clouds to complement the rest of the painting. Also, washing the sky across the trees and onto the landscape can often integrate the picture more successfully than when the sky is added first. However, this

▶ *Detail of the finished painting.*

▲ The wider landscape beyond the town.

◀ Pieces of paper painted in a selection of colours.

◀ Courtyards provide a cool refuge.

Materials for my collage

For my collages I use a sheet of mounting board, preferably '6 sheet' acid-free, backed with brown paper as a balancing veneer. I mark on it the size of the picture, leaving a margin, and fix it to a drawing board with drawing pins. I generally use Ingres paper in various colours as my medium, but you can use any good-quality paper; I sometimes work on handmade Japanese paper.

To ensure permanent colour as well as subtlety, I paint the paper with artists' watercolours, white designers' gouache and, sometimes, coloured inks. In this way I can create my own colour palette for the picture in progress.

Other requirements specific to the collage artist are a good pair of pointed scissors, a craft knife, glue or heavy-duty wallpaper paste, newspaper, blotting paper, tracing paper, soft cloth and paper tissues. Also needed is something to smooth out the pasted paper, such as a ruler or plastic set square.

▶ *Christine's drawing of the ramparts helped her to look hard at the subject and make decisions on the composition.*

The Method

◀ The first step was to draw in the main elements before small pieces of collage were applied to build up the sky, tree trunks, walls and background hills.

Having prepared my board, I paint my papers. For my collage of this Moroccan scene I needed a bright blue sky, so I painted the paper I was using with blue watercolour. When it was dry I dabbed it with a sponge loaded with pale blue gouache. Other colours required for the project are:

1 Reddish-browns for the walls – Burnt Sienna, Raw Sienna and Burnt Umber, mixed with Alizarin Crimson and Yellow Ochre.

2 Dark colours for the trees – Lamp Black, Hooker's Green Dark, Prussian Blue and Burnt Umber.

3 Light and dark greens for foliage – Lemon Yellow and Hooker's Green Dark.

4 Dark shadows – Lamp Black with Prussian Blue and Alizarin Crimson.

5 Very soft grey-greens for the hills.

6 For the flowers, some vibrant pinks and purples, using coloured inks.

The right composition

The composition is simple and is based on horizontal bands to evoke tranquillity. The ruined tower is the focus, while trees add a balancing, enlivening verticality. Even though I sat on the top of the ramparts while I did the initial drawing (*left*), the mountains dominated the tower. The bulk of the tower lay below me, with giant palm trees rising from the base of the walls.

▲ *Working on the picture as a whole, Christine adjusted shapes and colours to retain the balance.*

I started by roughly drawing the main elements, and then laid on the blue for the sky. Next I began to build up the collage, using fairly small pieces to form the tree trunks, the walls, the background hills and the palm tree leaves.

I worked over the whole picture, first laying in the general colours and tones until the white ground was covered. After that it was a matter of working around and around the picture, keeping hold of the structure. As you do your collage, take a good look at the shapes and adjust them if necessary, studying the drawing or other sources of the picture. Build up the layers, retaining a balance of colour and contrasting shapes. The dark shadows play an essential part in conveying the quality of light, and it is also important to make the mountains recede behind the ramparts.

I continued to add more and more of my pieces of paper, altering shapes and adjusting colours to create the effect I wanted. As the picture became more complete I added the greens in the right-hand corner, the flowers,

the foliage of the palm trees and finally the birds, wheeling in the sky. The birds in Morocco were plentiful, and the dawn chorus coming from the courtyard next to our bedroom was impossible to ignore.

I hope that my collage gives a sense of the immensity of the space that surrounded me. In comparison to the diffuse treatment of the mountains, the detail of the Roman tiles running as a stringcourse below the coping to the parapet was picked out to add interest, intricacy and an additional horizontal motif.

▲ **Ramparts, Hotel Palais Salaam, Taroudannt**
Collage
44 × 46 cm
(17½ × 18 in)
The use of hot colours and luxuriant greens evoke the sunbaked atmosphere and tropical foliage of this Moroccan scene.

9

The Project
Painting summer greens

Stanford Gibbons

Stanford Gibbons sets the challenging task of painting a predominantly green subject without using green in his painting

As the summer months approach the days become warmer and the sun continues to shine late into the long evenings. For many artists this is the perfect scenario for outdoor painting. Unfortunately, there is often a price to pay in that the gentle colours and transparent landscapes of spring are replaced by the dense opacity of summer greens.

In this project I want first to discuss the general problems of greens in the landscape and then set as a project the unusual challenge of painting a very green scene without having any green in your painting or on your palette at all. This will not only give you a real mind-bending problem but will also help you to gain a much better understanding and appreciation of greens and how to tackle their seemingly overwhelming predominance at this time of year.

Greens in your palette

On my courses many of my students tell me that other tutors have advised them not to carry any ready-made greens in their palette but always to mix their own. Though I do not totally agree with it, I can understand why this advice is given. Most ready-made greens are extremely unnatural and, if used directly onto the painting, can be disastrous. Many beginners exacerbate this by including a number of different ready-made greens in an attempt to create a variation that in fact results in dreadful colour clashes.

Study the subject before choosing the colours you will use and restrict them to a few. If you do have greens in your palette, always mix them with another colour when tackling natural greenery to achieve a realistic match. To avoid clashes, do not jump from colour to colour. For example, if, after considering the make-up of the greens in your subject, you choose to mix them with a combination of Hooker's Green Dark,

▲ *The cottage.*

◀ *The river.*

Cadmium Yellow Pale and Burnt Sienna, do not be tempted (except for rare and carefully considered exceptions) to use any other combination or addition. Permutations of two or all three colours will provide an infinite variety of harmonious greens.

This is just an example; you must select the appropriate colours for your painting, which need not necessarily include a ready-made green. If you maintain this discipline there is no reason why you should not have ready-made greens in your palette. Indeed, some greens can be quite difficult to mix when you do need them. I have Cobalt Turquoise Light among my watercolours; it is rarely any good for nature's greens, but I find it invaluable for many other things.

▲ *The old wall.*

◀ *The woodland.*

Green without green

You will see that I have selected four photographs, each of them a mass of deep summer green. The objective of this project is to choose one of the photographs and re-create it with no green at all in either your painting or your palette. To do this, you must select colours that will match the mood you wish to create and represent the greens they are replacing.

The reason why there are so many different shades and hues of green in the photographs is that each green is affected by another colour. The challenge is to identify that colour. For example, in the photograph of the cottage (*opposite*), the grass to the left of the cottage is clearly a pale yellow-green, so instead of a pale yellow-green, paint pale yellow.

You can use any medium you wish for this project, although if you choose watercolour, beware of the danger of unintentionally creating green when working wet-into-wet. Do remember to think through your composition and tonal values before starting your painting. Work out your ideas with quick thumbnail sketches and consider how the composition of the photograph can be improved in order to create your own interpretation of the scene. Instead of basing your picture on one of my photographs you could, if you wish, go outdoors and do the exercise *en plein air*.

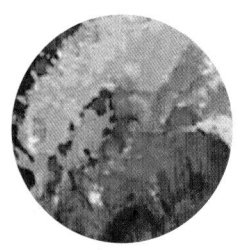

The Method

Although your challenge is to re-create just one of the four photographs on the previous two pages without using green at all, I decided to tackle all four photographs with different media and here you can see how I went about it. It is a pity that it is not possible to see and compare our work, as I am sure we would realize what an enormous variety of successful and imaginative ways had been employed to overcome the problem. However, thinking about greens in this analytical way will give you a much better understanding of the colour and greatly enhance your use of it in the future.

The cottage

In working out my composition I decided to reduce the depth of foreground and omit the tree and shrubs on the right in order to create a better balance and to give more prominence to the cottage. Additionally, I extended the background hills to the right rather than retaining a large area of sky. This is a gouache painting on Saunders Waterford

▼ **The Cottage**
Gouache
21.5 × 26 cm
(8½ × 10¼ in)
Reducing the foreground and foliage has established the cottage more firmly as the focal point.

Rough 614 gsm (300 lb) paper. I chose this heavyweight paper to support the heavy applications of colour.

Using the methods I explained earlier, I replaced greens with the colours that I considered were the hues affecting them. For example, if I thought that ochre was influencing a particular green, I painted it ochre; where I thought that deep blue was the main element of the green, I simply painted deep blue, and so on.

The river

In this scene, I liked the way that the large rock, which is about 3 m (10 ft) high, seems to dominate everything around it. I decided to emphasize this in my composition by closing in and omitting the outer areas of the photograph. I also liked the light showing through the bottom of the trees on the left of the rock, so I have made more of this and brought it closer to the centre.

In avoiding the use of green I have substituted colours that allowed me to create a feeling of the surrounding atmosphere, rather than rigidly adhering to the closer analytical approach. The water here has a reddish colour derived from mineral deposits on the rocks below the surface and this seems to reflect into the surrounding shadows, so I interpreted the scene in this way. I worked in watercolours on Bockingford 300 gsm (140 lb) stretched paper.

▲ **The River**
Watercolour
20 × 28 cm
(8 × 11 in)
Here a palette of reds and browns has replaced the greens of trees and grasses.

The old wall

The old tree and tumbledown dry-stone wall were what attracted me to this subject, but the main elements were too far apart. To overcome this I brought the two trees closer together. In the photograph the front wall creates a visual barrier, so I have made the gap more obvious to allow the viewer's eye to pass easily into the picture. I have also tightened the composition by leaving out the near foreground and the area to the right.

For this picture I reverted to analysing the different greens in order to decide my substitute colours. I worked in mixed media on stretched Bockingford 300 gsm (140 lb) paper. I started by loosely drawing the scene with acrylic ink applied with a dip pen. I then floated a variety of wet-into-wet washes of watercolour over the entire surface. This was followed by opaque areas of gouache and further drawing, using different acrylic inks.

The woodland

For this picture I chose to work in pastels on Schoellershammer pastel paper. I liked the compactness of the woodland and the straightness of the tall trees, so I emphasized this by closing in on the centre of the scene and making the composition a portrait format. The path in the photograph goes out to the left but I moved this towards the centre of the painting to give a better foreground lead-in. I also liked the glow of light at the end of the path contrasting with the dark woodland, so I tried to make this an important focal point.

I interpreted the greens as blues, violets and pinks, partly because I saw these as the appropriate substitutes and partly because of their proximity to the complementaries of the colours I used for the tree trunks. This counterplay enhanced the illusion of distant light in the painting.

▲ **The Old Wall**
Gouache, watercolour
and acrylic ink
23 × 29 cm
(9 × 11½ in)
*In this painting greens
have given way to the
colours that were
affecting them.*

▶ **The Woodland**
Pastel
40.5 × 28 cm
(16 × 11 in)
*Blues, violets and pinks
have replaced the greens,
paling towards the
background focal point.*

10

The Project
Atmosphere in studio landscapes

Norman Battershill

Norman Battershill demonstrates how to use your imagination to create a variety of atmospheric effects

Capturing a fleeting moment of light or an effect of weather when painting outdoors is not always possible or practical. In the studio, away from outside distractions, there is the opportunity to create a variety of atmospheric effects from your imagination. Success depends on how much you have learned from working outdoors and, of course, on your painting skills. Having the ability of visual recall is of primary importance for studio landscapes. This is achieved by studied observation of the ever-changing moods of nature, which becomes a daily habit and gives great pleasure.

The world's greatest landscapes have been painted indoors. For the finest examples of atmospheric landscapes and marinescapes, J M W Turner has no equal. His watercolour jottings were the seeds for his masterly studio paintings of nature's powerful forces and misty atmospheric effects.

John Constable's tiny outdoor pencil tonal sketches of his beloved countryside were the basis for many of his 1.8 m (6 ft) canvases painted in the seclusion of his London studio. Such genius is rare, but the lesson to be learned from these and other masters is that successful studio landscapes have their beginnings outdoors.

Using photographs

Photographs are a useful source of reference and a starting point for our studio project. My photograph is of a small corner of a Dorset field near my studio. This delightful area is a tiny segment of a vast expanse of open landscape beneath the vault of big skies.

Concealed by the undergrowth on the left, a quiet stream winds away into the far distance. Following its course across the fields at any time of the year, whatever the weather, gives me great pleasure. Carrying my pochade box and a sketchpad makes my travels easy.

The advantage of working from your own photograph is that you can probably recall the time and place. My photograph is of a location unknown to you, but the project is not to copy it but to use your imagination to create an aspect of weather and atmosphere, turning to it just for reference.

I used soft pastel for this project, although you can make your own choice of medium. Before you begin, spend a little time considering what you want to do. Have you any ideas for a new composition using the basic elements? Can the composition be improved? The post on the left is much too near the edge. I would be inclined to delete it or move it into the picture.

The sky is the keynote and determines the effect of light on the landscape, so change the flat sky in the photograph to a more interesting effect. Let your imagination run free as you work.

◀ *The subject for this project is a small corner of a Dorset field located close to the artist's studio.*

The Method

I have done six pictures derived from the main elements of the photograph, creating different moods in each. Before starting to paint, I decided to simplify the foreground and the left-hand side of the photograph. The trees were spiky and too forceful for the kind of schemes I had in mind.

In all the paintings and sketches I began with the sky. When the mood of the sky had been roughed in I established the tone of the landscape to ensure harmony. Both landscape and sky were then progressed together.

In my first painting (*above*) I wanted to achieve the effect of a bright clear day with a

▲ **Dorset Fields 1**
Soft pastel on almond pastel velvet card
20.5 × 28 cm
(8 × 11 in)
In order to simplify the subject, Norman opened up the foreground and made more of the partly hidden stream on the left. The trees on the left-hand side were deleted altogether to achieve recession.

▲ Dorset Fields 2
Soft pastel on almond
pastel velvet card
20.5 × 28 cm
(8 × 11 in)
*In this painting
Norman created the
effect of a frozen stream.
The black trees are the
darkest tone and make
a linear contrast to the
flat expanse of sky.*

fresh after-the-rain sky. To help judge the tonal values more easily, I roughed in the blue of the sky first, and then the clouds. The horizon also provided a key to the tone of the landscape, which I made dark enough to give light to the sky.

For the second painting (*above*) I decided upon a snowy scene with a frozen stream. In the middle distance the russet colour of the sapling is an accent of warmth. Teasels from the photograph are included in the foreground. For this subject I was unsure at first what to do with the sky, then decided that a flat sky of mauve would give warmth to the proposed snow scene. Having laid the pastel on the board I rubbed it in firmly with a rag to achieve the effect I had hoped for.

Direct approach

For the first three paintings in this project I worked with soft pastel on pastel velvet card, the surface of which gives bite to pastel. Mistakes are not easily rectified, but that encourages a more direct painterly approach. The general composition can be lightly

roughed in with a piece of natural charcoal that will blend with soft pastels. Alternatively it can be dusted off, but care must be taken not to damage the surface.

In the third painting (*above*), the season has changed from winter to the kind of summer day where soft rain and gleams of sunlight create a rapidly changing and evocative landscape. To encourage the eye to move into the painting, part of the hedge on the extreme left is blurred. A glimpse of sunlight at the end of the hedge is a focal point, and rain in the distance further enhances the atmospheric effect of the scene. Instead of teasels in the reference photograph, cow parsley and buttercups create interest in the foreground.

Moving or deleting parts of a subject when painting outdoors can create problems of composition. In the studio, greater attention can be given to the structure and development of a painting, and I was able to move and change things in the photograph after considering the composition. The advantage of creating an imaginary setting

▲ **Dorset Fields 3**
Soft pastel on almond pastel velvet card
20.5 × 28 cm
(8 × 11 in)
For this subject Norman has included only the trees in the foreground. Sunlit clouds and rain falling in the distance evoke a day with shadows and gleams of sun moving over the landscape.

▲ Dorset Fields 4
Soft pastel on
smooth card
12 × 22 cm
(4¾ × 8¾ in)
The scene still has the
same elements but has
now become one of a
landscape bathed in
the gentle light when
colours have begun to
fade a little.

from a reference is that you can alter it in any way you like, perhaps into a different subject altogether.

The fourth painting (*above*) is included as an example of soft pastel applied to smooth white card. Blue and lilac are blended in the sky by rubbing with a kitchen tissue. A full moon at dusk is the theme, but the landscape is still filled with that magical half light between day and evening. The subject of dusk and dawn has many variations. With my sketch painting here I can completely change

**▶ *Detail of* Dorset
Fields 4.**

the mood of the subject simply by making the landscape a darker tone.

The last two pieces of work that came from this project are charcoal sketches. The first (*above*) explores the accents of light and dark that can give life to a landscape painting, and could well be the basis of a large finished work. The second (*below*) is a further exploration of the way in which the photograph can be translated into an entirely imaginary subject. Charcoal sketches should, of course, be fixed instantly on completion to avoid smudging.

I hope that this variety of work will have encouraged you to make your own explorations of what you can find from a subject. All you need is something to trigger your imagination. Putting it into practice is the hardest part!

▲ **Dorset Fields 5**
Natural charcoal on smooth paper
6.5 × 12.5 cm
(2½ × 5 in)
This charcoal sketch makes further use of the trees that appear in the reference photograph, but as in all these pieces of work Norman used his imagination as well.

◀ **Dorset Fields 6**
Natural charcoal on smooth paper
7 × 9.5 cm
(2¾ × 3¾ in)
Another small charcoal sketch employing the elements of the photographic reference to form an atmospheric subject. Charcoal drawings are a very quick way of developing an idea and are excellent for establishing the tonal harmony of the piece.

11

The Project
Still life in watercolour

Lesley Hollands

Lesley Hollands shows how careful grouping and lighting will help your composition, setting the mood with china, lace and fabric

I have always enjoyed using china as a subject and find the delicacy of aged porcelain a fascinating subject. For this project I have chosen a variety of china that I have collected over the years from junk shops, jumbles and car boot sales. None of it is perfect. With this I have put some fabric and flowers.

Starting points

Gather together several pieces of china that you find interesting. Choose some coloured or patterned fabric that complements your china, plus some white cloth or paper.

Setting out your composition on a low table or on the floor will enable you to see into the cups. Surround your group with the coloured fabric to avoid difficult decisions about what to do with empty background space.

Lay the white cloth or paper on the fabric to make an interesting shape, then start to arrange the china. Odd numbers grouped together are more pleasing to the eye than even numbers and triangular shapes within the group give a stronger composition. Be aware not only of the shapes of the objects you have chosen but also the spaces between them.

Once you are happy with the grouping, light it with an anglepoise lamp or something similar. The way the group is lit will make a lot of difference to the composition. Low lighting gives longer shadows, which can connect objects that are not overlapping. If it is too low, though, you will not light the inside of the cups, while too high a light will give pools of shadow and flatten the insides.

Sketch your composition, taking care to get the ellipses right. Putting two straight edges next to an ellipse will make you more aware of the shape (*see diagram*). Looking at the drawing upside down or in a mirror can also help you to see any mistakes. Once you are happy with the sketch you can start to paint.

▲ *Gather together more china than you will need so that you have plenty available to choose from.*

◄ *Odd numbers grouped together are more pleasing to the eye than even numbers.*

The Method

For my still life I selected two pieces of white fabric, a colourful old summer frock and some cups with a variety of patterning. I also chose to put some white flowers into the composition to give greater height and add a soft-edged element. The group was set up on a low table and lit from the right-hand side with a table lamp.

Establishing the colours

I started by drawing the cups with some care, getting the spacing, perspective and ellipses right, before sketching in the flowers and the edges of the white cloths. The flowers were painted first, just in case they died or were disturbed by one of my cats. I then started to put the detailed pattern on the cups, trying to get the colour just right first time in order to avoid over-working and losing the crispness of the hard edges of the china. I chose to put in the darkest cup first to act as a key point. Other tones were measured against this.

Next came the lace pattern on the white cloth. The lacy effect was achieved by painting the spaces between with varying shades of pale blue and ochre. The colours needed to be kept light to avoid making the lace look too solid or heavy and to keep it

▲ *Lesley started by drawing the cups, adding colour to the darkest cup first to act as a key point by which to measure other tones.*

▶ *Detail from the drawing above.*

◀ *Take care with your ellipses. Putting a straight edge near the ellipse will help you to be more aware of the shape.*

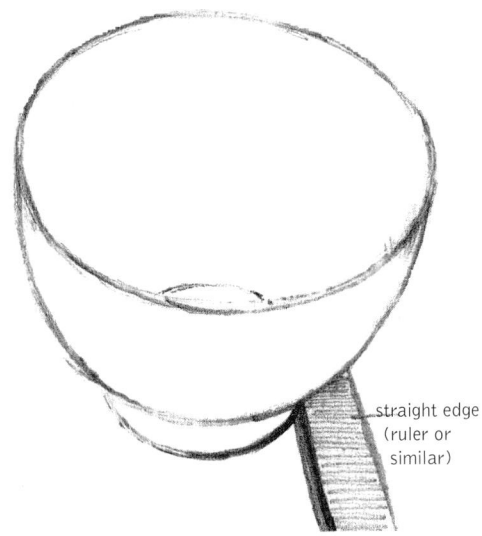

straight edge (ruler or similar)

The colours of the patterned fabric were added freely to give a general impression rather than with careful detail, which may have been too dominant.

from playing more than a supporting role in the overall composition. After this I started to put in the colours of the patterned fabric, working quite freely and trying to give a general impression rather than careful detail, which might have become too dominant in the composition.

Keep checking the balance

At each stage I propped up the painting and stood back from it so that I could judge the balance of the composition and see, and

▲ Returning to the painting after a couple of days, Lesley made some adjustments to the patterned cloth and the white fabric. She also sharpened some of the shadows near the base of the cups.

correct, any mistakes before I progressed any further with them.

Once the cups, flowers and fabrics were laid in I started to work on the shadows, which are a very important aspect of the painting. They have a lot of subtle colour in them where light has bounced off other coloured areas, and they help to describe form and position. They show, for instance, that the cups are hollow and the fabric is not smooth.

When I reached this stage I left the painting for a couple of days without looking at it. Going back to it with a fresh eye, I noticed a number of things that I felt needed to be adjusted. The patterned cloth was too pale and did not offer enough contrast to the white, so some of the sparkle had been lost. Also the back edge of the white fabric was too clearly defined, which made it jump forwards rather more than I felt was right. To correct these faults I applied much stronger colour to the patterned fabric and let some of it run over the back edge of the white cloth. I then strengthened and sharpened the shadows near the base of the cups and made a slight correction to the front ellipse. After leaving it again for a while, I finally felt satisfied with the finished result.

▲ **China, Flowers and Lace**
Watercolour
38 × 45.5 cm
(15 × 18 in)
In the finished painting, stronger shadows and colours gave dynamism and sparkle.

12

Mother and child in oils

John McCombs

John McCombs
sets a classic subject for this project and suggests oils as the painting medium

The subject of this project is my partner's daughter, Pip, with her baby son, Michael. I shot a full roll of film to capture the right moment and chose this pose to paint as I felt it had all the ingredients for a good life painting in oils.

I suggest that when attempting this subject you should first of all consider the composition. You may, for example, wish to close up on the facial features and hands of mother and baby. Personally, I like the complete figure, which I feel gives a fuller sense to this classic subject.

I asked Pip to wear the red dress because of its rich colouring, and as the fabric is quite thick, the folds and creases give a fine sculptured sense to the underlying forms. I also asked her to clothe the baby in light colours so they would stand out tonally against the red dress.

As she was seated in an extra-large armchair she was able to pull her feet up onto it, thus creating an interesting angular movement through the body from head to foot. The natural light from the window picks out some strong linear qualities, whereas in other areas edges are lost in shadow, particularly around Pip's back.

Keep it simple

It is always best to try to avoid imitating patterns or textures as these may detract from the more important aspects of form and features. Also, do not feel the need to capture an exact likeness of mother and child; this is a figure painting, not a portrait. Keep the faces simple, particularly the baby's, and as soon as a sense of form has been achieved in both, leave them. With regard to the rest of the subject, imagine you are making a piece of sculpture, cutting into the finer areas with a smaller pointed brush and modelling the broader areas with a larger brush.

Initially, keep the oil paint thin and let it build up as the picture develops. Work with confidence and be prepared to make mistakes; these can always be painted over or scraped away later. Give your attention to the qualities of light, form and space occupied by the figures and above all keep the painting alive.

◀ *Photograph of Pip and her baby son, Michael.*

The Method

◄ This close-up reveals the very free handling of the paint.

Although I have advised you not to copy the facial features of the subjects slavishly when you paint this subject, for my own part I felt I wanted to create the likeness of both mother and baby in my picture as they are members of my family. Nevertheless, I still treated the subject as a figure painting and not as a portrait.

Composition

Before starting I considered the composition. I wanted to include the full length of the seated figure as I felt it created an interesting movement throughout the painting. I was happy for the mother's shoe to be slipping out of the picture as this adds interest to the movement and suggests that reality exists beyond the frame. I also decided to simplify the background so that it did not detract from the main theme and this included the removal of the radiator from underneath the window.

The light coming into the room flooded the subject from a single direction, giving a great sense of form to every aspect. The shape of the extra-large armchair, which supports and encompasses the figures, invests the subject with a feeling of occupied space that is also helped by the obvious lines of perspective.

I was pleased to find that the material of the mother's red dress was linen so when she sat down the folds fell in chunky formation over her body, creating a sculptured effect, which did not necessarily follow the underlying forms of her figure. Her dark hair, the red dress and the light colour of the baby's clothes made a rich scheme of colour and tone against the neutral surround of wall and chair.

I was keen to avoid interpreting any kind of textures in the painting, be they pattern or material, and preferred the idea of allowing the texture of the paint to provide the interest. I believe that part of the pleasure of studying any work of art is in seeing how the artist has used the medium. I knew my painting was going to be based on sound draughtsmanship, so this was the point from which the painting started.

Starting to draw

I decided to keep the head well up to the top of the composition and began, from that point, to draw the shapes with my No. 2 brush and a turpsy mix of dark-toned oil paint. I drew quite freely, establishing proportions while knowing that they would probably be changed time and again. Before the whole of the composition had been fully resolved I began to push in some colour with my No. 5 brush.

I felt it was important to keep the appearance of the painting changing in order to stimulate ideas. When a picture remains static for a while it can begin to look uninspired, so I kept the oil paint liquid to the point of runny at first, knowing that layers would be built up as the work progressed. As well as using my small brush to draw, I imagined myself to be sculpting with it, which gave the line a different quality. When working with larger brushloads of pigment I sometimes saw it as coloured clay with which I was modelling the forms.

The close-up detail on the previous page reveals that the paint is handled very freely. The drawing of the mother's arm and hand supporting the baby's head was a joy to interpret.

I was pleased that this subject offered a complete range of tones, from the dark colouring of the mother's hair, which was painted quite flatly, to the extreme contrast of the baby's light clothing.

I knew the main treat in store was going to be painting the red dress. This was gradually built up with brushloads of paint being pushed and pulled over and around the forms as can be seen in the detail above. At times when the paint got unmanageably thick, the knife was brought into play to scalpel away any displeasing mounds of pigment. This is a technique that I have employed for the past ten years or so and I find it useful for releasing exciting undercolour to enliven a dead area.

Mother and Child was drawn, painted, scratched and repainted, scraped and painted yet again, with every brushmark being based on the true realities of light, form and space. This approach was maintained with vigour and confidence until the final picture presented itself.

▲ *Brushloads of paint were pushed and pulled over and around the forms.*

▶ **Mother and Child**
Oil
44 × 33.5 cm
(17¼ × 13¼ in)
A tender subject, painted with vigour and sculptural brushstrokes.

A Greek scene with acrylics

Wendy Jelbert

Wendy Jelbert explains the techniques for using acrylic paints, choosing a Mediterranean subject for her example

Acrylics are increasingly popular and many students particularly want to learn how to use them. An acrylic painting can resemble a watercolour or an oil painting with equal success. However, some students complain that the medium dries too fast or that the colours are too bright and gaudy. The quick-drying quality of the paints can indeed be a problem to start with if you are a slow worker, but this can be overcome with practice. If it continues to be a problem, a retardant can be added.

The colour chart for most brands of acrylics is now the same as for watercolours and oils and a very extensive range of gorgeous colours is available. Acrylics are also long-lasting and adhesive. You can varnish and frame a picture on the same day you have painted it.

The size of the picture I have painted is 28 × 38 cm (11 × 15 in). The brushes you will need for the experimental chart (*below*) and the painting are a soft 13–19 mm (½–¾ in) flat brush; a hoghair or round-headed brush (size 10) and a rigger (size 14). You will also need a stay-wet palette. You can buy this or make your own by placing a wetted tissue in a shallow waterproof container topped with greaseproof paper to place your paints on. When it is not in use clingfilm can be put over the top.

Paints and supports

Paints can be bought in a starter pack, tubes or pots, the most well-known brands being Winsor & Newton, Daler-Rowney, Liquitex and Talens. The colours you will require for this project are Olive Green (Hooker's Green will do), Yellow Ochre, Burnt Sienna, a dark blue, a dark brown and a grey, plus white and Cadmium Yellow. Alizarin Crimson was mixed with blue for shadows.

You can apply the paint to any support such as paper, cardboard or canvas. I used a heavy Not surface watercolour paper, stuck to a board with masking tape.

▶ *Techniques with acrylics.*

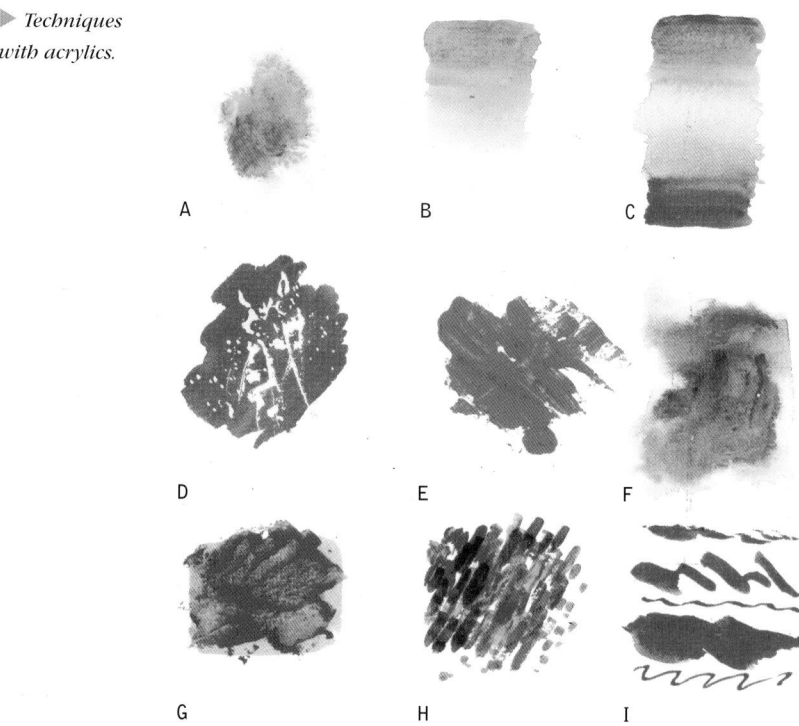

A

B

C

D

E

F

G

H

I

▶ *Each year I take some students to a different Greek island. Last year we visited Paxos and this was one of the delightful sights we found.*

Techniques with acrylics

If you are a beginner with acrylics you need to explore this medium before you start the project. Try out the techniques used in the chart shown on the opposite page. Keep on experimenting until you feel confident about your handling of the medium. You will then feel able to paint with your attention focused on composition, tonal values and colour relationships.

A If you want to treat acrylic paints like watercolours you have to be lavish with your use of water. Here, I wetted the surface and dropped in watery acrylic paint, as in the wet-into-wet watercolour method.

B and **C** I graded one colour with water, then added another colour and graded it.

D I used masking fluid on the surface then washed over it with thin acrylics. When the paint was dry I exposed the white paper by rubbing off the mask.

E This effect was achieved by applying thick paint with a palette knife.

F Similar to **A**, but with two colours. I rocked the paper to mix the paint.

G Here I applied one colour on top of another and allowed the bottom colour to gleam through.

H and **I** These examples demonstrate some of the effects that can be achieved by laying different colours on top of each other and using brushes of various widths.

◀▲ *The goats were constantly in motion, so we took photographs for reference as well as sketching them.*

While photographs provide a useful reference for studies of animals, particularly if they are moving at high speed, they are no substitute for doing some quick sketches before you incorporate the animals into your composition. The act of making some simple, unimportant drawings will enable you to explore their form and movement in a relaxed way, and your finished painting will benefit from your resulting familiarity with your subjects.

▲ *Wendy made a series of sketches of the goats.*

The Method

Before I started upon my painting I did a series of thumbnail sketches in which I moved the focal point of the composition to various positions.

Establishing the focal point

The focal point of your composition should hold the darkest, lightest, most colourful and most detailed point in your picture. I suggest that when sketching out this painting you put some masking fluid on some of the stones, perhaps around the door and windows.

Care should be taken in how the windows, door and trees are placed in relation to each other. If you are going to put a goat in your painting, remember that it will draw the viewer's eye, so its placing is also important. The feeling of rhythm and movement in the mounds of the stones should also be taken into consideration.

While you are painting your picture, especially in the early stages, use the paint in light washes and build up to thicker layers. This is particularly important in the trees and bark and the textural differences of the stones and foliage.

The shadow cast across the left-hand window of the farmhouse and under the trees should be added last as a gentle glaze in blue and violet. This will add drama and a feeling of sunlight to the picture. Try to maintain the contrast between the sunlit façade of the building and the dark, almost silhouetted left-hand tree.

◀ *Different focal points are tried out in these thumbnail sketches.*

▲ Wendy's information sketch, showing her colour notes.

Beginning the painting

Once I had established my thoughts about the focal point and composition I did a sketch of the scene (*above*), giving information about colour, tone and texture for future reference. I also took more photographs to help me with some sketches later on.

Next I prepared my heavy watercolour paper with a drawing to sketch out my focal point of the goat and the dark tree (*opposite, top*). I also pulled the left-hand window towards the right-hand side, leaving more space on the left; there should always be a still area of at least 10 per cent to offset the activity in the rest of the picture.

With masking fluid I highlighted the goat and parts of the foreground with the left-hand olive tree, plus some details of the tiled roof and tree branches. I also placed in the details of the door, windows and some of the grasses among the stones.

▶ A sample of assorted pastes and gels. B, C and E are mainly sandy surfaces; A and D are the smoother pastes; in F, eggshells have been pressed into a smooth paste surface.

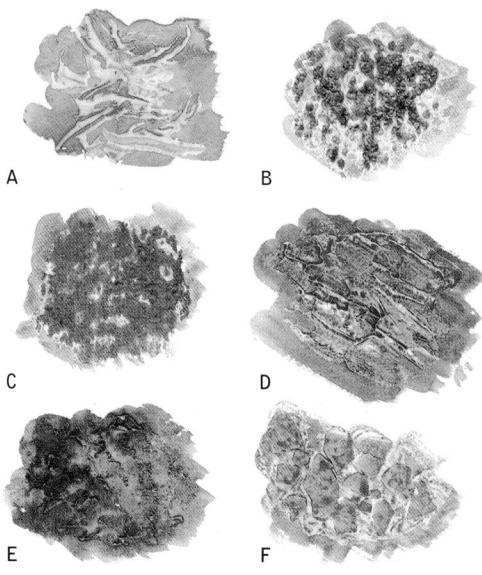

Assorted surfaces

For the more experienced among you, I feel that adding a textured paste to the stones in the foreground and the sunlit façade would be beneficial and a bit of fun. Textured pastes are available in pots and are mostly made by Winsor & Newton, Liquitex and Daler-Rowney, but you can explore textures further by mixing in eggshells, as I did in an experimental fashion (*below*). In this painting of a Greek scene, I used a fine sand paste which was deposited on the surface in thin blobs with my palette knife then allowed to dry thoroughly.

I next used my large brush to apply the first watery wash of Yellow Ochre to the façade of the house and over the stones. This should be your next step, whether or not you have used the texture paste method.

While this is still wet, drop in strong washes of Burnt Sienna across the foreground on to the right-hand side, sweeping towards the left-hand corner and under the left-hand window to give a warm, sunny glow. Use dark green above the roof and across to the left-hand side of the tree. I mixed the basic green with some brown while adding more blue to the olive tree foliage. While the paint was still wet I dropped in some bright yellow just above the central window. I filled in the windows and door using the blue and Burnt Sienna watered down.

I mixed a little grey, using blue and Burnt Sienna. (You can buy a ready-mixed neutral grey which is very useful.) Dropping blobs of the grey on to the stones gave a little depth to their structure. I also started to detail the stonework on the house front, using my rigger brush and dark brown paint. The right-hand tree was painted with a round-headed brush and Burnt Sienna.

The finishing touches

As you reach the final stages it is always a good idea to prop up your painting and view it at a distance. This often pinpoints any mistakes at an early stage.

Using thicker and bluer paint I placed in the olive tree foliage with small stabbing marks of the rigger. Then I painted in the details of both trees and some of the stonework with light and dark browns. After this I rubbed off the masking fluid and washed in the white areas with Yellow Ochre and pale blue.

The tiles and some of the grasses were painted in with Burnt Sienna and Yellow

The early stages of the painting.

▶ **A Greek Scene**
Acrylic
28 × 38 cm
(11 × 15 in)
Warm colours and textured pastes give the feeling of weathered stone in a hot climate.

Ochre. When all was dry, I mixed Alizarin Crimson, blue and a touch of Burnt Sienna for the shadows and placed them carefully under the eaves and across the façade, the stones and the goat. These accentuate the structure of the steps, door and windows and give drama and contrast to the painting. Finally a little highlight of thick yellow ochre and white was added to the stones with a palette knife.

The beauty of using acrylics is that you can build up the paint using watercolour and oil methods in one picture without it getting too muddy. In this painting of rural Greece I used gentle glazes and thicker paints, giving gentleness and strength in one picture. I hope that the project will inspire you to try out more complex subjects using acrylics and textured paste.

14

The Project
A cottage garden in line and wash

Alan Oliver

Alan Oliver imagines what the great British painter J M W Turner would have made of this quintessentially English scene

I am always happier using line and wash on buildings rather than for open landscapes, and this traditional cottage and garden is a subject that in my view would work well with this technique. If I am using black ink for the line, I try to blend it or hide it in parts with very dark tonal areas. I do not like the outline to dominate, simply being filled in with weak washes of colour, like an illustration in a comic.

The light in this photograph is very boring, and it requires some drama injected into it. As you can see from my tonal sketch (*below*), my way of doing this was to reverse the tones, with the sky becoming darker than the walls and roof of the building. I always try to imagine what the great J M W Turner would have done with a subject such as this and I suspect that he might have chosen to do something similar.

In my sketch I have also altered the perspective a little in order to lower the eye level slightly, and put a curve in the path.

Have some fun with this and see what you can come up with. On the following pages you can see what I did with it.

◀ *The subject of this project – a traditional rural scene.*

▶ *Alan's tonal sketch. Reversing and strengthening the tones has added drama to the scene. The perspective has also been lowered and the path curved to lead the viewer's eye into the painting.*

The Method

◀ *Delicate watercolour washes were applied before the ink lines.*

Using the photograph and sketch as a guide, I decided not to do the black ink lines first but to pencil the positions in roughly and start with washes of fairly light tones instead. I deliberately did not try too carefully to keep within the pencil lines, and I also decided to use one brush throughout – a blunt No. 16. It is only blunt because it is old and really worn out!

I worked on Bockingford 300 gsm (140 lb) unstretched paper, which was just lightly attached to a board with four small pieces of masking tape at the corners. The colour range I used included Indigo, Coeruleum, Indian Yellow, Yellow Ochre, Cadmium Red, Alizarin Crimson, Burnt Sienna, Sepia and Sap Green.

Applying the ink

When the first washes were dry, I tried a little ink line work using a Pentel Brush Pen. This is a nylon-tipped pen with waterproof ink in a cartridge, which produces a lovely range of marks depending on the pressure applied – from delicate to bold. The other pen lines were made using a hard nylon-tip pen No. 5.

▲ *A little line work was added with a Pentel Brush Pen.*

◀ The dark colours in the windows were varied to stop the house from looking dead and empty.

▼ Splattering paint across the foreground suggested a busy cottage garden.

▲ Another wash of Indigo helped to make the cottage stand out.

As you can see, I did not apply the outline everywhere – mainly just on the sides where the shadows fell. Another wash of Indigo in the sky helped to bring out more light on the cottage. I varied the dark colours in the windows in order to give a sense of the cottage being lived in. If all the windows had been black, it would have looked empty and dead.

A few rich darks helped to swallow the black lines, while shadows brought out the sun. Finally, I used a pointed brush and white ink to paint in the window bars. It is much better to use this method rather than try to paint each window pane at this small size.

The garden was handled very loosely, giving the appearance of a generous abundance of flowers and shrubs. I also used a good deal of splattering to give an impression of a busy cottage garden.

I hope you have enjoyed this exercise as much as I have. Remember, do not simply copy photographs; draw inspiration from them and use your imagination.

▲ **The Cottage Garden**
Line and wash
28 × 38 cm
(11 × 15 in)
Alan's choice of colours suggests mellowed walls and a traditional cottage garden.

15

The Project
A quayside scene in oils

Harley Crossley

Harley Crossley
concentrates
on shapes
and colours
in order
to create an
abstract painting
of a rainy
industrial scene

I am fortunate enough to spend a good deal of time travelling the world on cruise ships, lecturing and demonstrating the technique of knife painting. Some of the most interesting scenes to paint *en route* are the busy docks, with the hustle and bustle of cargo being unloaded, cranes moving ponderously along the quayside and containers being lifted on and off the decks of giant vessels.

The photograph shown here is of the docks in St Petersburg. It was taken on a cold, showery afternoon when all the workers had gone home, leaving a silent expanse of containers and storage sheds with cranes towering over the scene.

This is an interesting composition but it is too jumbled to make a pleasing painting. I decided to simplify it radically and use it as the basis for an abstract painting. The contrasts between the vertical lines of the cranes and the horizontals of the containers and sheds really excited me, especially where the bright colours of the containers occur in the foreground.

Look for shapes and colours

My abstract paintings are based on actual scenes, but I abstract areas and shapes that I feel are essential to make a pleasing composition. It is usually still possible to recognize the source of my inspiration. Because it is not always easy to simplify what you see, I suggest that you look at the scene with your eyes half closed. This will block out the inessentials, leaving only the dominant shapes in view. Try to see the scene as a series of shapes and colours. You can then use these as the basis for the painting.

I worked in oils applied with knives for this project, painting straight onto a primed, stretched 30.5 × 40.5 cm (12 × 16 in) canvas. I based my colours on those shown in the photograph, but you may think that it would be more abstract to change the colours completely. Indeed, it would be an interesting exercise to paint the entire composition in shades of brown or grey for a monochromatic effect. These are the choices you must make before you begin to apply paint to your canvas.

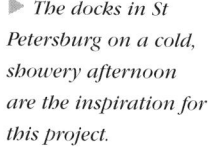

▶ *The docks in St Petersburg on a cold, showery afternoon are the inspiration for this project.*

The Method

▲ *With his oils squeezed out onto his palette, Harley was ready to begin the painting process.*

▶ *The shapes of the containers were suggested by scratching the paint with the tip of a worn small knife.*

Painting an abstract does not come easily to me as I like to paint what I see, so this project was an interesting exercise for me – as I hope it will be for you.

Before I began to paint I made a conscious effort to empty my mind of my memories of the bustling dock scene I had watched before the workers left for home that afternoon. I concentrated instead on the shapes and colours in my photograph, looking at them through half-closed eyes.

Beginning work

Having made the decision as to which colours I would use for my painting, I squeezed my oils out onto my plastic palette in readiness to begin work. Because I paint onto a white canvas, I always use a white palette so that the colours look the same on both surfaces.

Using the flat blade of my large knife, I covered the top area of the canvas with a mixture of Titanium White and Alizarin Crimson, followed by a band of light Payne's Grey, and blended the two areas together with the flat of the knife. I then used my finger to scumble the colours together more thoroughly. Next I scraped off as much of

this paint as I could, leaving only a thin layer on the canvas, which created an almost translucent effect.

With the edge of the blade of the large knife I then painted in the vertical lines from left to right, inspired by the cranes in the photograph. Ignoring the roofs of the sheds that account for quite a large area of the photograph, I concentrated instead on the shapes that were made by the containers. The small knife was ideal for these. By loading the knife with paint and then pressing the flat of the blade directly onto the canvas I could get the size and shape I needed quite simply. Once I had painted all of these I employed the tip of my worn small knife to scratch into the paint and create edges to each one (*above*).

For the foreground I used similar tones to those at the top of the canvas but made them slightly darker. By mixing Payne's Grey and a touch of Alizarin Crimson into the Titanium White I achieved the slightly opaque shade that you can see in my first attempt (*top, p. 76*). This shows the completed painting, but I was not very happy with it. I felt that it was still too recognizable as a dock scene so I had another go.

▶ *The artist's first painting of the docks, which he considered to be too representational.*

▶ *On a second attempt Harley built up the paint in the same way as he had previously, using a wet-in-wet technique.*

▲ *The colours on the sheds and containers were applied in groups.*

Wet-into-wet oils

I use the 'wet-into-wet' technique of painting. This means that I start at the top of a canvas and work down, finishing each area as I go, laying wet paint over the top of the wet paint already there. The disadvantage of this method of working is that it is difficult to go back into a painting and alter anything done earlier.

So, making a fresh start, I loaded my large knife with a mixture of Titanium White and Alizarin Crimson once more and swept it across the top of a new canvas. Again this was followed by Payne's Grey and the colours were blended as before and then scraped off. I was happy with the colours I had used previously, so I saw no reason to change them.

Using the edge of the large knife, I drew the straight lines over the area already painted, wet-into-wet – you can see how difficult it would be to alter the background colour at this stage. Some of the shapes made by these straight lines were then blocked in with colour using the small knife, again painting over the colour already on the canvas.

The blocks of colour came next. Now was my chance to use Naples Yellow, Cadmium Orange and Prussian Blue to give the painting a lift. Prussian Blue is a very powerful colour and I always employ it with care. Mixed with white or Payne's Grey, it is much more manageable than when it is used straight from the tube. It is all too easy to find that what started out as a touch of colour to give

contrast or highlight has taken over the painting and it has ended up as a symphony of Prussian Blue.

Notice how I have used my colours in groups, beginning with the blue on the left-hand side of the canvas, through the yellows and oranges to the brown and back to blue tones on the right and in the foreground. The remaining area of canvas on the left of the picture was painted using a mixture of Payne's Grey, Titanium White and Alizarin Crimson, balancing the tones at the top of the canvas. Using the small knife for this area, I was able to suggest texture with the ridges of the paint as it came off the knife.

The canvas was now completely covered with paint and in a landscape painting this would be the end of my work. However, because this was an abstract I felt that I needed to link the areas together more. This necessitated working back in the middle of the painting – a thing that I never normally do. By loading the edge of the large knife with paint, I drew more lines across some of the blocks of colour, linking the uprights into them.

I hope that you enjoyed working on this project and found it a challenge. I know that I did. For me this is what painting is all about – enjoyment and the continual exploration of new ideas.

▲ **The Docks at St Petersburg**
Oil
30.5 × 40.5 cm
(12 × 16 in)
Simple forms and strong colours have created a powerful painting.

16

The Project
A still life in watercolour

Moira Grice

Moira Grice helps you to make the most of your subject. Select your still-life objects carefully for the best possible arrangement

Fruit and vegetables make wonderful still-life subjects. Ideal, I thought, for a painting project, especially if you were asked to arrange them within different formats. My photograph (*below*) shows a variety of produce, which I deliberately did not arrange into any particular composition. The two rough sketches (*opposite*) show how I have selected certain items from the group and arranged them into both landscape and portrait formats. This is how I hope you will approach your picture having, of course, first read my advice and been alerted to some of the likely problems.

The landscape format illustrates how the halved pepper, tomato, bananas and apple all add some interest and colour to the rather bland appearance of the other vegetables. However, the composition looks rather overcrowded and unimaginative. A possible solution is to focus on just five or six items from the group, placed close together, and enlarge them sufficiently to fill the entire picture area.

The same produce has been arranged in a portrait format, although some of it does not fit comfortably into this dimension. The shapes of the spaces between the objects have altered quite dramatically and I now feel that the entire subject appears to be floating in space. The answer might be to reduce the format – make it slightly shorter and wider – or eliminate a couple of the items altogether.

Some words of advice

Use the two sketches as a starting point and produce several sketches of your own in both formats until you create a satisfactory composition. Remember to:

1 Avoid concentrated areas of warm or cool colours. Instead, disperse them evenly over the picture.

▶ *Choose some of the fruit and vegetables from this photograph and arrange them into landscape and portrait formats.*

▶ The carrots and half mushroom have been eliminated from this landscape format arrangement. However, the composition still looks overcrowded and rather uninteresting.

2 Build up the watercolour washes until you have achieved the desired colour and tone.

3 Pay special attention to the colours and tones of shadows within the spaces. Their purpose is to link the items together and to create the impression that they are resting on a solid surface upon which their colours are reflected.

4 Keep the spaces between the shapes and the expanse of background as small as possible. This will help to prevent the still life from appearing weightless.

▶ In this portrait format the produce appears to be floating in space.

The Method

▲ These small, rough thumbnail doodles show how the ideas for the final composition were developed.

Preparatory sketches

To the layman, my thumbnail doodles (*above*) must appear as unrecognizable scribbles, but to me they are a valuable form of brainstorming. Their purpose is for me to generate, develop or scrap ideas prior to starting my preparatory line and tonal

sketches. Through this series of thumbnail sketches I have selected, discarded and arranged the produce into different landscape and portrait dimensions. Gradually, an idea began to emerge that I was able to develop into the final composition.

With any composition there should be a balanced distribution of objects, shapes, colour and tonal values. As my preparatory colour drawing (*below*) demonstrates, the bold colours of the cut pepper, apple and tomato provide some much-needed contrast to the rather bland appearance of the cauliflower, leeks and parsnip. However, the natural curve of the top leek is central to the entire composition. It encourages the eye to wander naturally from the bottom left corner to the top right and, together with the strategically placed onion, links together the shapes and colours of all the items.

The painting process

Having transferred the composition onto Bockingford 300 gsm (140 lb) Not surface watercolour paper, I placed a very light watery wash of Gamboge (Hue) and French Ultramarine over the cauliflower, leeks and apple. Gamboge (Hue) and Cadmium Red Deep were then added over the parsnip, onion and pepper, and Gamboge (Hue) and Alizarin Crimson were put on the tomato. While these washes were drying, I mixed a thicker consistency of yellow/green, which comprised more Gamboge (Hue) than Coeruleum, and a much darker mixture of French Ultramarine and Gamboge (Hue). The latter wash was applied only to the dark green shapes on the cauliflower leaves and leeks, revealing the yellow/green wash underneath to suggest the veins and light areas.

Mid-tone washes, comprising Gamboge (Hue) and Cadmium Red, were painted onto the pepper, onion and tomato. Once they had dried, I mixed and overlaid a thicker wash of

◀ Moira's preparatory coloured sketch.

the same two colours, plus a little Alizarin Crimson to make the rich dark areas on the pepper and tomato. Gamboge (Hue), Cadmium Red and a little French Ultramarine produced a warm brown for the onion and the detail on the parsnip.

Alizarin Crimson, together with French Ultramarine, was also used for the apple's skin and subsequently for its reflection in the shadow. The highlight was removed with clean water when this wash was still damp.

Shapes, shadows and detail

Light is falling directly from the right, which means that the spaces between the objects are in shadow. The lightest shadow, for example, the one closest to the source of light, is underneath the pepper. It is made up of orange – Cadmium Red Deep and

Gamboge (Hue) – mixed with just enough complementary blue (French Ultramarine) to make a warm grey. Using complementaries in this way, in varying proportions, enables the colour of the object to be reflected in the shadow. The same colours have been used in different proportions to reflect the tomato – a little Cadmium Red Deep added to a dark blue/green mixture of French Ultramarine and Gamboge (Hue) – and the apple, where a little Gamboge (Hue) was added to a red/purple mixture of Alizarin Crimson and French Ultramarine.

I then placed a thin yellow/orange wash on the remaining background areas. Finally, I defined each object with a small amount of detail, using thick colour mixes and a No. 2 brush, and assessed and corrected the colours and tonal values where necessary.

17

The Project
Changing the perspectives of a Kentish lane

Aggy Boshoff

Aggy Boshoff encourages the use of multiple viewpoints to liberate your work, drawing from the example of the artist David Hockney

In this project I shall be encouraging you to experiment with changing perspectives to see what it can do for your painting.

Take a look at this composite image of a country lane in Kent (*below*). I use this lane several times a day, by car and on foot, because it leads to the house where I live. I consider myself lucky to have such splendour on my doorstep, and it is this elation with the world and with nature that motivates much of my painting. I know that this is the case with most of you too.

I would, of course, like to preserve forever the golden light that floods in and creates such a riot of colours as well as those strong opposites of lights and darks. Attempting to do just that, I took a photograph, or rather a series of three photographs without moving from the spot – just turning around a little to the right after each shot. I then pasted the photographs together, slightly overlapping each other.

The British artist David Hockney has done this many times and I would like to discuss this aspect of Hockney's work – namely the great things he has done with perspective and photographs.

The composite photograph, showing the view of the lane to the artist's house.

More than a single viewpoint
Hockney believes that naturalism is a trap from which one has to escape. He admires the Cubists in general and Picasso in particular. The single viewpoint perspective, which was invented by the Renaissance and is continued today by the photograph, was considered by the Cubists to be an illusion. Their way of seeing and understanding an object properly was to walk around it and to experience it emotionally as well as optically.

Hockney realized the dilemma that perhaps the only time photography can be completely true to its medium is in using it to make reproductions of paintings, when the flat surface of a painting is reproduced on the flat surface of the photograph. In 1982 he began to make Polaroids and photo-collages. One such photo-picture is *David Graves, Pembroke Studios, London, Tuesday 27 April 1982*. It consists of 120 Polaroid photographs assembled in a grid to form a larger image of a figure seated in an interior. Each Polaroid records its image frontally and in focus. When assembled to form the composite image, everything in the picture, whether foreground, middle ground or background, is seen close up on a shallow plane defined by the camera's focal length.

It takes time to make a series of photographs such as these, but it also takes time to view them. The seemingly impersonal eye of the camera becomes the vehicle for a personal involvement in the accumulation of a sensual experience. Hockney has illustrated this element of time with an analogy pointing to Chinese landscape, which is an art of time as well as space. As the eye proceeds from right to left, the scroll is unfolded on the left as it is folded up again little by little on the right.

With one-point perspective we restrict space to a single vista, as if seen through an open door. The Chinese depict a space as though they had stepped through the same open door and then felt the breathtaking experience of space extending in every direction and infinitely into the sky.

The Method

Although I find it difficult to move away from the familiar one-point perspective, it is painting with multiple viewpoints I am asking you to experiment with. It should give you an enormous feeling of freedom – a feeling that anything is allowed.

I have been experimenting with triptyches painted on MDF for some time now. You can buy sheets of MDF measuring 1.2 × 2.4 m (4 × 8 ft) at the timber yard and have it cut down to smaller sizes to fit your requirements. For this scene I used three panels measuring 1.2 × 0.6 m (4 × 2 ft) each. The idea of using several panels is to make each one of them interesting in its own right, but for this project it is immaterial whether you paint on one panel or more. My panels are framed individually and hung no more than 5–7.5 cm (2–3 in) apart.

I work as follows. In the first session I paint the entire panel with colour, no matter how vague or wrong. Then, with as big a brush as I can muster, I go over the whole painting again, concentrating on the darker areas – in this case the shadows of the trees on the banks and the road. The colours of the shaded areas are very important to me. Any purple, from the red spectrum to the blue, sets off the predominantly green and yellow of the picture very well.

Although the colour of the picture is quite naturalistic, I wanted to overdo the sunny effect of the scene, so I emphasized the lemon yellow in two or three leafy areas of the painting. I also splashed yellow over the ground where it bursts in from the gaps between the trees on the left. Although it was autumn when I painted the scene and I was

▲ **View Down the Lane**
Oil, triptych
1.2 × 1.8 m overall
(4 × 6 ft)
Abstract brushstrokes and a heightening of the yellow emphasize the sky and sunlight in the scene.

in the studio working from photographs, I experienced the same urgency I would have felt had I stood out there in the road, with the threat that the sun was about to disappear and take my image with it.

The brushstrokes in the painting are abstract. It is really all to do with applying colours in the right places. At a fairly early stage the sky has to be indicated. For this I used two brushes almost simultaneously. One brush was loaded with the pale blue of the sky and the other with the colour of the

▲ **The Lane**
Oil
48 × 60 cm
(19 × 23¹/₂ in)
This was painted from the same position as the triptych on p. 83, but this time the artist has included the orchard and house in the distance. Although she was unable to see them, she was aware that they were further down the road.

leaves. The two brushes were exchanged between the painting hand and the other hand in quick succession until the sky started to shimmer through the leaves. The larger leaves on the right-hand panel received a dark green edging in most places, to make them clearer and to allow them to work as a foil for the rest of the painting.

Move into your painting

Have a good look at Hockney's famous work of 1980 – *Mulholland Drive, The Road To The Studio*, which is reproduced in the books *David Hockney, a Retrospective* by Christopher Knight, et al (1988) and *That's The Way I See It* by David Hockney (1999), both published by Thames & Hudson.

However, only face-to-face can one fully experience the impact of this enormous 2.1 × 6 m (7 × 20 ft) canvas, which was painted from memory in three weeks. Hockney knew the road well because it led to a studio he kept for some time in Santa

Monica. 'You drive around the painting', Hockney says, 'or your eye does, and the speed it goes at is about the speed of the car going along the road.' Following the curving road, the eye absorbs a great variety of motifs, each forming a focal point of its own. No attempt has been made at unified perspective – in fact the vantage point shifts constantly.

In *Principles of Chinese Painting* (1959), George Rowley wrote: 'By this device one might travel through miles of landscape, might scale the mounting peaks, or descend into the depth of the valleys, might follow streams to their source or move with the waterfall in its plunge. How wonderfully our apprehension of nature has been expanded, combining in one picture the delights of many places seen in their most significant aspects. Such a design must be a memory picture which the artist created after months of living with nature and absorbing the principles of growth until the elements of landscape were "all in his heart". Then, and then only, could he freely dash off hundreds of miles of river landscape in a single scroll in which the design evolved in time like a musical composition.'

I have tried to paint a single picture of the entire lane from memory, and one from the same vantage point as in the triptych on p. 83, both with changing viewpoints (*right and left*). It is Hockney's aim to create a clarity of space: a space that is playful and moving. With this play of space, time and memory, he wants to make the viewer participate. Do my efforts succeed in this aim?

Hockney says it is our movement that tells us we are alive. His collages hold four possibilities of movement:

1 The subject is moving.

2 The artist's glance is moving (the triptych on p. 83).

3 Both the artist and the subject are moving.

4 The artist is moving (*above left and above right*).

The photo-collage *Pear Blossom Highway, 11–18th April 1986*, is the final development of Hockney's work in this respect. It is a combination of photography, painting and collage. The picture in part illustrates Western one-point perspective: the road vanishes into the middle of the horizon. But by showing

other perspectives as well, Hockney states that this one has no precedence over the others; it is simply the driver's choice, while the passenger may gaze elsewhere – at the litter along the road, for example. Space is made wider than is possible with a single shot of the camera or a single perspective painting.

Reverse perspective

The effect of movement is the creation of 'reverse perspective'. The viewer moves about the object, seeing it from one side, then the other; coming up close, then looking down on it. In traditional perspective, infinity is a long way away and you can never reach it. However, if you reverse perspective, infinity is everywhere and you are part of it. There is a vast difference in the two viewpoints and a totally different way of looking at the world. Hockney is drawn to modern physics. He recognizes a connection between one-point perspective art and Newtonian physics, which sees the world as existing outside of us. The

multiple perspectives used by him and the Cubists also have a connection with the physics of Einstein, who makes any measurement relative to the observer.

The traditional Renaissance perspective is by no means the 'natural' one. Look at how a child draws a picture. They depict whatever they want: the front, the side or the back of a house, the backyard tree and the duck pond down the lane. Wrong, we say. You cannot see all these things at once. Do it this way instead. We are wrong, however, and the child is right because in fact we do not perceive reality in single perspective. The child's version is more alive and ours a more impoverished rendition, because the child incorporates the piece of paper painted on as well, and translates onto paper. Traditional perspective looks through the piece of paper as if it was not there.

I find the second and third paintings more child-like than the triptych, but they were enormous fun to paint. Set your memory working and try the project again!

▲ **The Lane, 2000**
Acrylic on board
58 × 75 cm
(22³/₄ × 29¹/₂ in)
The entire lane, with its surroundings – a house, a pond, and orchards along the road.

18

The Project
Coastal scene painted in watercolour

David Bellamy

David Bellamy takes us to Angle on the Pembrokeshire coast and shows how to make the most of light with watercolour

Angle, at the western end of Milford Haven, is one of my favourite subjects. If you stand near the middle of the muddy harbour (preferably when the tide is out), you are almost surrounded by subjects. After a line of mature trees comes the church, some cottages and then the old ruined tower with the stream coming in; more cottages and then the scene shown in the photographs (*below and right*), the whole sprinkled with a fair selection of boats of various shapes and sizes. And, of course, there is the mud to top it all.

I have chosen the end cottages, beyond which the shoreline turns back towards the Old Point House, a pub much frequented by pirates in earlier times.

Assessing the scene
The two photographs were taken within an hour of each other and show the same scene from slightly different angles, but with contrasting moods set by the stunning light catching this very edge of Pembrokeshire. Wellies were the order of the day, in order to traverse the mud and get into the optimum position for sketching.

The first photograph (*below*) reveals the subject bathed in sunlight as the tide recedes. I chose this time as I prefer the tide to be low or halfway in, rather than have water everywhere. A slight breeze disturbed the water horizontally, breaking up the reflections, as if made to order. A dark sky accentuated the whiteness of the cottages although, as you will see from the second photograph (*right*), the right-hand cottages are not white at all. Few subjects make perfect compositions, however, and what disturbs me about the first photograph is the random scattering of boats, the green ranks of vegetation to the left of the buildings and the long straight lines of the harbour wall, which is actually a track to the left of the cottages.

The position I took for the second photograph enabled me to capture some old stumps of rotting wood – the broken ribs of ancient vessels, the remains of which are revealed in the mud at low tide in places.

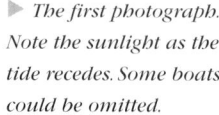 *The first photograph. Note the sunlight as the tide recedes. Some boats could be omitted.*

A lighter sky shows that the cottages are darker than was suggested by the first photograph.

These give some foreground interest and will suggest depth in the final painting. The stream runs through this view and there are several mini-creeks here and there which can be useful aids to lead in towards the focal point. Again, the boats are not perfectly placed and the harbour line is very strident. The lighting does show up the tree at the right-hand end of the cottages more clearly in this photograph. When the scenes are viewed together they illustrate the importance of taking a number of photographs in addition to your sketches.

Reaching a decision

So that terrifying moment has arrived – a decision has to be made. Do we make the cottages or the boat serve as the centre of interest, or perhaps something completely different? Think about employing some of these features as a support to the others. Consider the positions of the boats. Should they be moved farther into the picture, closer to the side, or closer to the cottages? Should the sky be dark or light against the buildings? What sort of atmosphere have you in mind – warm, cool, dark, light, rainy or sunny?

Here, the lighting is full on the front of the cottages, but you may wish to have it coming from the side, or even above. As Constable said, 'The sky is the source of light in nature, and governs everything', so choose your sky treatment with care. Do those reflections

inspire you? If you decide to include them it might be a good idea to break up the foreground a little with those lovely dollops of dark mud as a contrast. Think about ways to break up that straight line across the centre of the picture. Consider also including some life in the form of seagulls or figures to add interest.

The important thing is to be sure about all the above considerations before you touch the paper. In order to help you with this, I suggest that you carry out a few rough thumbnail sketches in pencil or charcoal to give yourself an idea about where to position each main element, and also where the strong light and dark tones will appear. No one can paint lovely, fresh watercolour washes on paper that has been ravaged by a thousand rubs of a pencil eraser. You might even like to cut out little paper boats and move them around the paper until you find a pleasing composition. Once you are happy with the layout, transfer the drawing to the watercolour paper.

Consider using a tinted paper for this subject. The painting can be effectively carried out on white paper, of course, but it will be interesting for you to see how your watercolour techniques respond to tinted papers. You might find it a fascinating exercise to try one painting on tinted paper and another on ordinary white paper then compare results.

The Method

The outstanding advantage of working from photographs in the conditions I found myself on that November day in Angle harbour was that they froze the lighting effects, which were constantly changing. Under these circumstances, sketching or painting *al fresco* becomes quite a challenge, but it does make you tackle the most vital elements within the scene in a robust manner. Although on this occasion we are working directly from photographs, do bear in mind that there is nothing quite like working in front of nature to help you learn to paint. A pencil study of a rotting gatepost set amid the chaos of brambles, thorns and weeds is worth a thousand photographs of the Bacino di San Marco to the aspiring artist.

If all the readers who participate in this project were in my studio we would probably find that no two paintings of the same scene would be alike, so do not expect your composition to end up similar to mine. We all place different emphasis on the various features within a composition, so such variation is perfectly natural. However, take some time to analyse the difference between my approach and your own – the reason for the inclusion or positioning of certain features, and what techniques have been used in order to obtain certain effects.

The first stage

In my response to this subject I established three critical stages in the development of the painting. Basically, I used the second photograph as my prime source and injected some of my own flavouring here and there, as I feel it is important to stamp something of yourself on a painting.

The paper I chose to work on was Bockingford Grey, a tinted 300 gsm (140 lb) paper with a Not surface. In the first stage (*below*) you can see the initial washes of colour. They are a mixture of Monestial Blue and Indian Red (I often use more powerful colours than normal when working on tinted

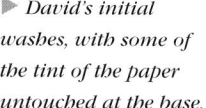
▶ David's initial washes, with some of the tint of the paper untouched at the base.

papers) with just the tint of paper showing on the lower part.

Setting the composition

I decided to make the cottages the focal point and to support them with boats drawn up close by rather than scattered around, which would be distracting. By including one of the weed-dripping, rotting spars near the foreground, a sense of depth would be imparted, the spar adding foreground interest without overwhelming that area. I elevated it slightly more than appears in the photograph. Just beyond, I intimated a little creek to suggest a lead-in towards the buildings.

Generally, I aimed for a gloomy atmosphere punctuated by strong highlights of sunlight breaking through, but with distant hills subdued within the gloom. The source of light would come from directly above the focal point. In order to reduce the impact of the strident line of the top of the harbour wall it would be played down considerably.

Tackling the sky

I began with a weak mixture of Monestial Blue and Indian Red, defining the distant ridge to the right of the focal point. When this was dry a stronger version of the same mixture was applied over most of the sky, keeping a clear patch in the middle sky and introducing Naples Yellow just above the cottages to highlight them. Because Naples Yellow is quite opaque, it is a useful colour on tinted papers, as it can effectively kill the tint in places.

When these washes were dry I brought some Permanent Rose into the clear patch of sky, slightly darkening it lower down by introducing a hint of the main sky wash. At this stage, the stronger cloud above the buildings was painted in, again with the main wash mixture. Some Raw Sienna was then brushed into the area below the cottages and into the foreground and allowed to dry.

The stronger tones were created from a mix of Monestial Blue and Burnt Umber. This was used on the trees, with the dark vegetation being brought down to define the left-hand wall, which was mainly the Raw Sienna applied earlier. A sloping bank leading down in front of the buildings was suggested. This was substituted for the track which is strongly etched across the photographs to where it links up to the top of the harbour wall.

▲ *The watercolour is complete apart from the highlights. Compare this with the final version on p. 91 to see how important it is to bring out the highlights on a tinted surface.*

▲ Detail of the finished watercolour.

The harbour wall itself was made less prominent, softened even more as it moved away from the focal point, and broken up by the masts of the boats drawn up on the foreshore. With dry-brush technique, where there is little water on the brush, I streaked broken colour across the more distant part of the flat muddy bed of the harbour, reinforcing the effect with the odd darker blob in places.

Losing edges

Once the painting was dry, another dry-brush passage was placed over the stream, making sure the right-hand side was kept clear to suggest the lighter water, and the left-hand side dark to reflect the gloomy sky above. The small side-creek below the boats not only leads in towards the cottages, but breaks up the long line of the farther bank of the stream. You can also see in the finished picture that the lines of the banks of the stream are accentuated in some places and almost lost in others.

When all was dry the strongest tones were brushed into the foreground detail areas and some detail was hinted at with a few dark marks here and there. When I applied some spatter with a toothbrush it went completely awry, as the low trajectory meant that the spatter was flung across the surface of the water I wished to keep clear. Happily, most of this disappeared when washed with a large wet brush. With a No. 1 rigger, I drew in the masts, telegraph poles and a couple of gulls hovering close to the focal point.

Bringing out highlights

The painting was then ready for the final stage – applying the highlights. Unlike white watercolour paper, where the lightest tone is the paper itself, tinted papers need an uplift to create real sparkle. Beware of adding white paint at an earlier stage, as it can mess up any colours with which it comes into contact.

I re-wetted the top of the cloud-window and dropped in some white gouache so that it softened as it moved outwards into the damp patch, to suggest the lighter sky. Then, with hardly any water on the brush, I drew in the white highlights on the cloud edges. With a No. 4 round brush, blobs of barely moist white paint were dragged across the flat area below the cottages and boats to suggest the sparkling mud and pools of water. I added a few blobs here and there, and finally rendered the fronts of the cottages with weaker white gouache to complete the painting.

As you can see, the grey tint shines through the transparent washes, unifying the scene. Although I have not done so in this painting, the paper can be left unpainted in places, as the Bockingford tints are not fugitive when exposed to light. Conversely, it may be necessary to kill the tint in some areas, as with the Naples Yellow in the sky above the cottages, in order to provide a contrast. The choice of tint depends to a strong degree on whether you need a warm or cool overall feeling in the work.

I hope that you are now inspired to look more closely at mud, for in the right light it can be more beautiful than all the treasures of a royal palace. If you tried this subject on white paper, why not repeat the exercise on a tinted paper such as Bockingford Grey or Blue. If you did use a tinted paper, have a go at it on white paper. Tinted papers demand a slightly different approach and are excellent in helping you to get out of those painterly ruts we all suffer from every now and then.

▲ **Angle, Pembrokeshire**
Watercolour
28 × 38 cm
(11 × 15 in)
Here the highlights have been inserted using white gouache to add sparkle to the painting.

19

The Project
A disused farmhouse in pastel

John Patchett

John Patchett warns readers not to copy the photograph but to improve upon the composition and use their own creativity

This old farm building, which has obviously been left in a dilapidated shape for some considerable time, stands proudly above a very flat landscape, making a clearly defined silhouette against a large sky. At the time the photograph was taken, sunlight lit the scene from the left to give the building and the old hay bales a strong three-dimensional quality.

In order to translate the photograph to a successful pastel painting I knew a number of adjustments would have to be made to the composition. At the moment the eye is too easily drawn to the left-hand side of the picture. The dark tone of the end gable and the shaded side of the round bales would also need to be made much lighter. Other considerations were whether to make the barn even more dilapidated by crumbling parts of the roofline, raising the pitch of the roof, and letting part of the sky appear through the window in the end gable.

Producing a tonal sketch

Making a sketch is an important stage as it is the time when most of the thinking, decision-making and development of your initial ideas

▲ *The old farm building, isolated in a flat landscape.*

takes place. A tonal study, in which particular attention is paid to counterchange, is essential in order to help carve out the composition and structure of your painting. It also allows you to place dark and light tones next to each other, define shapes and work out how to take the eye on a journey into the picture. Converting a photograph to a small sketch also helps you to eliminate unnecessary details that may prove a distraction to the viewer's eye.

The study I did in my A5 sketchbook (*above*) was produced using a Karisma Graphite Aquarelle pencil, which is an ideal medium for sketching. As it allows you to go over some of the shaded areas with a soft wet brush it also gives you the option of producing tones. You can therefore work quickly, creating a loose watercolour effect, while at the same time emphasizing the main tonal values.

As you can see from my sketch, I decided to keep the majority of the foreground in shadow. This allows the viewer to look past the darker tones towards the centre of the painting and then follow the lighter areas in front of the barn, in and around the hay bales and eventually on towards the horizon. I have added an extra-large hay bale and a tree on the left-hand side to help the overall composition and to create a focal point on the distant horizon. You might like to consider suggesting one or two details of your own in the foreground, particularly on the left-hand side.

Lastly, I injected some atmosphere into my finished piece of work by means of bleaching out the horizon, adding soft sunlit clouds in the sky and replacing much of the green grass with golden straw-coloured glazing and texture.

Good luck with producing your version of this isolated and dilapidated farmyard. Please remember that your task is not to copy the photograph but to use it to help you see a number of possibilities and to clarify your thoughts about it. Produce a small sketch of your own, even if it only takes you five or ten minutes. I guarantee that during that period of sketching you will make a number of key decisions that would not have been possible any other way.

There comes a time in any painting when serious and careful analysis is required as to what there is left that still needs to be done. It is all too easy to overwork a pastel painting, so take good care that you stop before you do so.

My own pastel painting derived from my sketch and photograph of the farm buildings was made on a 30.5 × 43 cm (12 × 17 in) sheet of golden ochre pastel card. I used this particular background colour in order to help to bring out the warmer colours of the scene and emphasize the sunlight.

▲ *John's initial tonal study, executed with a Karisma Graphite Aquarelle pencil. The light and dark areas of the scene have been simplified. The composition was also altered where necessary.*

The Method

▲ The initial stages of the pastel painting. Willow charcoal has been used, with transparent pastel highlights.

Referring to my small tonal study, I proceeded to sketch in the composition lightly with a stick of willow charcoal. Then, using the side of the pastels, I loosely placed transparent layers of Lemon Yellow (0) and French Ultramarine (0) over some of the light areas. By now the bones of my pastel painting were established and I could start to build on them.

I decided to use mostly Daler-Rowney pastels for this project as they allowed me a good range of colours with excellent handling qualities.

Keep it moving

Always avoid the temptation to press hard or 'finish off' areas prematurely. I started blocking in areas with delicate transparent layers, making sure that the painting was kept in a loose, changeable state by working on as many areas as possible at the same time. The darker areas, such as the end gable, the shadows next to the bales and barn and the front corners, all needed to be kept to a medium to dark tone, so I used transparent layers of Purple Grey (4) and Red Grey (6).

The tree was similarly treated with a glaze of Terre Verte Hue (8) and the bales of hay with Autumn Brown (5). Touches of Olive Green (7), which is a warm earth green, helped to bring the foreground forward.

The middle distance, which I found to be the most exciting area to concentrate on, required clean, brighter hues and confident handling. The bright side of the building was painted with Cadmium Red Orange Hue (3), Yellow Ochre (2) and Poppy Red (1). The ground in front of the barn needed to be kept relatively light in order to make a strong contrast with the dark bales. Cadmium Tangerine Hue (2) and Lemon Yellow (0) with touches of Raw Sienna (4) were used to retain a glowing sun-drenched feel, taking the eye diagonally across the composition.

At this stage the painting had lost much of its structure and parts of the drawing needed to be re-emphasized. Using Purple Grey (6), I put in the dark windows and doorway with the end of the stick of pastel to create a hard-edged mark. Accents were introduced under the eaves and against the bales, the posts, the gate and the corrugated tin sheets.

The sky, which I felt needed to be kept pale to contrast strongly with the building, was built up using the side of the pastel, with delicate transparent layers of Coeruleum (2), Cobalt Blue (2) and, towards the top, French Ultramarine (4). The clouds were Raw Umber (3), Purple Grey (2) and Lemon Yellow (0). For the roof, I used Cadmium Tangerine Hue (6) diluted with Poppy Red (1) as it receded. This gave a richness to the painting, as orange and blue are complementary colours.

The sunlight on the grass, tree and mounds of hay was put in with a slightly firmer use of Sap Green (5) and Yellow Ochre (4). To help create a feeling of space beyond the buildings, I used Grass Green (1) for the distant fields, and Mauve (1) for the horizon.

Adding detail

Using Olive Green (8) and Purple Brown (6) for dark accents and Lemon Yellow (0) for bright highlights, especially on the hay bales, brought the painting alive. Textural marks were introduced to the foreground with flecks of Cadmium Orange Hue (6).

Finally, using Prussian Blue (8), I added plastic sheeting to the left-hand side to echo the shape of the hay and take the eye back on its journey through the centre of the picture.

▼ **Disused Farmyard**
Pastel on golden ochre pastel card
30.5 × 43 cm
(12 × 17 in)
From a starting point of delicate layers of pastel, the artist has built up a painting rich with form and texture.

20 The Project
Autumn in the Lake District

James Fletcher-Watson

James Fletcher-Watson paints the mountains of Cumbria in watercolour, following a long-established artistic tradition of the area

The autumn is the best season for painting in the Lake District, and in fact this applies to any mountainous area of the British Isles. The colours are much better at that time, as can be seen in the photographs shown below. You find this view after travelling from Seatoller in Borrowdale over the steep Honister Pass and down into the Buttermere valley, with the fast-flowing stream (or beck, as it is called in Cumbria) and rocks forming a delightful feature.

I have chosen this view because it is a particularly good composition. The stream gives a pleasing foreground interest and the dark Scots pine spinney forms a helpful tone value for the scene. The mountains make a superb background. You will notice the roof of a building just showing against the pine trees. I decided to make a feature of this by raising it slightly and adding chimneys.

I also felt it might help to see a little more of the stream, so I tried moving closer to it. However, the water dominated a bit too much so I moved slightly farther back towards the mountains again for my final choice of view. You will see a single sheep in the first photograph, but I did not like its position so I moved it a bit to the left and added a second sheep. This is a legitimate ploy as we are artists, not photographers.

As I observed the scene I noticed some gaps in the clouds showing blue sky. This provided an opportunity to have cloud shadows in the foreground to help to give life to the picture. Cloud shadows on the mountains were also invaluable.

When you are making your own painting do not forget the really dark items, such as the banks of the stream, the stone walls, the shadows of the rocks and some of the trees. I think I have given you enough hints for you to get cracking with your own rendering of this lovely view, but you can also read exactly how I tackled the project and the colour mixes I used.

▲ *Gatesgarthdale, Cumbria, with autumnal colour.*

▶ *The same scene from another angle, showing more of the river.*

The Method

I decided to use a sheet of Bockingford heavyweight watercolour paper for my painting of this Cumbrian landscape. I began by drawing the scene with a 2B pencil. I chose the viewpoint already described and, as I worked, made other minor alterations which I will mention as we go along.

At the drawing stage, I slightly opened up the mountains on the left to make their tops more distinct and drew in two sheep in the foreground. I was then ready to start painting. To help explain the painting process the picture is shown at the halfway stage (*above*) as well as the finished work on p.99.

Various mixes

I started by painting the sky, first damping the area with clean water. With a mixture of French Ultramarine and Burnt Umber I ran a grey wash over the sky and right down to the foot of the mountains, leaving the area of blue sky and white cloud untouched to start with. While that wash was still damp I painted French Ultramarine where the sky was blue, leaving the sharp white clouds unpainted.

Next I dropped in a small area of Cobalt Blue just below the French Ultramarine, using this lighter blue because here the sky is nearer the horizon. When this was almost dry,

▲ *The painting at the halfway stage.*

I painted in some slightly darker grey clouds on top of the first grey washes.

Next came the background mountains. As you can see, these were various shades of brown and grey. For these I used various mixes of Burnt Umber, Burnt Sienna, Raw Sienna and French Ultramarine. I started with the left-hand mountain, working along to the right and ending with the very light, blue-grey distant mountain, for which I used a mix of Cobalt Blue and Light Red. The low cloud touching some of the mountain tops was achieved by introducing clean water with a separate brush.

I could then paint the sloping fields below the trees to left and right, using Raw Sienna and a touch of Cobalt Blue. When all was dry I painted in the various tree groups, using a smaller brush and a mixture of Burnt Umber and Winsor Blue. For the extra dark Scots pine trees behind the cottage I added some Payne's Grey.

The next step was to paint the typically Cumbrian dry-stone wall running right across the picture with a stiff, dry mixture of French Ultramarine and Light Red. I used a small brush, dragging it sideways and leaving little bits of white where stones were catching the light. I indicated the banks of the rocky stream with a mixture of Burnt Umber and French Ultramarine, again using a small brush.

▼ Detail of the finished watercolour.

Using artist's licence, I invented a dark bush halfway along the wall on the right-hand side in order to break the monotony and to draw the viewer's eye away from the farmhouse, which was left white at this stage. The timber drop-gate on the stream was painted with a very small brush and a dark brown colour. The picture was now about halfway to completion.

Sharp shadow

I tackled the second and final stage by first painting all the areas of field which, in autumn, were a rather dull yellow-green. I used Raw Sienna and French Ultramarine, carefully painting round the rocks and sheep, leaving them white. While the washes were still damp, I introduced some small bright green areas using a Cadmium Yellow and Winsor Blue mixture.

The rocks in the stream and on the grass were painted with a very stiff mixture of French Ultramarine and Light Red. This dark colour was for the right-hand side of the rocks, giving the sharp shadow caused by the sun, which was sporadically shining from the left.

Next, I painted the farmhouse, starting with the roof. Coeruleum mixed with Light Red gave a good grey for the Cumbrian slates. The right-hand wall was washed in with a Cobalt Blue and Light Red mixture, giving a suitable

shadow colour for white walls. The same two colours, but in a stronger mixture, provided the shadow under the eaves. The small window showing above the fold of the land was touched in with a Burnt Umber and French Ultramarine mixture.

The two sheep in the left-hand side of the foreground were painted with a very dark brown for the faces and legs and a warm yellow-grey for body shadows. I mixed three colours for these: Raw Sienna, Cobalt Blue and Light Red.

Then came the important stage of painting the water. With fast-flowing water you find white foam against rocks, so I applied a light wash of Payne's Grey and a touch of Raw Sienna, brushing it sideways across the stream and leaving white gaps in suitable places. At this point, I touched in a bush to the left of the trees and also put in some low shrubs a little higher up the mountainside, brown at this time of year with dead bracken.

Finally, I put in some cloud shadows over the fields, with a fairly dark one in the immediate foreground. These shadows were the colour of the fields, green on green and brown on brown.

The cloud shadows were also carried across the stream, using a medium dark mixture of Payne's Grey. A few tufts of grasses and reeds were added with strong green-brown mixtures and a few scratchings out with a penknife – and that concluded the painting work.

▲ **Gatesgarthdale, Cumbria**
Watercolour
38 × 53.5 cm
(15 × 21 in)
The use of colour, texture and cloud shadow makes this scene highly evocative of the Cumbrian landscape in autumn.

99

21

The Project
The riverside at Putney in oils

Ronald Morgan

Ronald Morgan demonstrates how to paint a narrative picture of the Thames, with boats and figures making for a lively scene

Painting rivers and canals has always been a wonderful experience for me. In particular I greatly enjoy working along the stretch of the Thames from Greenwich westwards to Putney. The riverside at Putney is a most interesting place, with the old boathouses, rowers, sightseers and so forth. The only problem for the artist is that people often leave their cars parked at the side of the road opposite the boathouses, thus blocking much of the view along the riverside.

On the day I took this photograph, a lovely July afternoon, there were fewer cars parked than usual, so I had a better view of my chosen subject. This is the spot where the university boat race starts from every spring. I have no doubt that some artists would include the parked cars in their paintings, but for this project I decided to concentrate on other elements of the scene instead.

Painting a story

Before commencing a painting I always make a number of very quick compositional sketches of the subject. It is important to juxtapose figures until you are satisfied that they are in the correct positions in the picture. In a subject of this kind, allow the figures to tell the story of what is happening. Paint them in such a way as to give a feeling of movement, as this will add to the atmosphere and interest of the work. Let the light and dark colours used in the painting capture the brightness of the afternoon and the warmth of a lovely summer's day.

There are no rules as to how many sketches you should make; sometimes it might take 20 sketches before you arrive at a satisfactory composition for the painting. Using the information given in the photograph, produce a small, quickly painted picture before you begin your finished work. There is blue, yellow and light red in this subject and white can be used to pick out the highlights on some of the figures.

▲ *The Thames at Putney is the subject for this project.*

▶ *Compositional sketches will help you to establish the best position for the figures and allow the light and dark areas to play their parts in capturing the atmosphere of the scene.*

The Method

◀ Quick pencil sketches of figures in motion are useful to place in your painting later.

In my painting, done on the spot, I wanted to convey to the observer the enjoyment that I experienced when visiting such a lovely place and to capture the atmosphere and vitality of the riverside there.

I began by producing a few quick pencil sketches of the buildings, the distant trees and other elements of the composition and made some equally quick sketches of figures walking by the river.

Beginning to paint

I covered a primed 23 × 30.5 cm (9 × 12 in) panel with a wash of very light Yellow Ochre and, using a small brush, drew in the general shapes of the buildings, trees and river. I washed in the darker areas with medium-strength dark blue paint, then I washed in the sky, but not the clouds, using Coeruleum near the horizon and French Ultramarine with a touch of crimson at the top of the picture.

After putting in the red-brown areas to the left of the subject I covered the whole of the foreground with purple shadow before deciding where to place the pools of sunlight within it. I wanted to eliminate the ragged edges of the shadow that appear in the photograph. I then concentrated on the lighter side of the trees facing the sun, using Yellow Ochre with a touch of Light Red. A darker colour – French Ultramarine with Yellow Ochre and Light Red – was applied to the right side and bottom of the trees to suggest shadow and to give a feeling of roundness and depth.

At this stage I spent a little time drawing the buildings in more detail and inventing a few objects in the left foreground to add more interest. I 'designed' the cloud formation in the sky as I feel that it is important to arrange the clouds in such a way that they relate compositionally to what is below them.

▲ *Here Ronald has placed his figures definitively in the composition before beginning the painting.*

◀ *Detail of the finished painting.*

I worked on the river next, taking note of the shadows on the surface of the water, and placed highlights on the few distant boats before tackling the figures. A group of rowers were chatting together before carrying their boat to the water's edge and launching themselves upstream. Other club members were already in their boat and beginning to row away.

Although the central figures in the painting were satisfactory from a compositional point of view, there would have been too much emptiness in the foreground without the two figures to fill that space and, hopefully, to add a little more interest to the work. As the central figures were important parts of the subject, I placed them in a pool of sunlight and added strong highlights to their clothing. Abstract shapes such as these in a painting will enhance and give dramatic effect to the overall image and beauty.

As the artist works he or she must always bear in mind that particular attention needs to be paid to colour harmony. The colours must relate to each other so that the overall effect pleases the eye. I hope that your efforts are successful and that you enjoy painting this subject as much as I did.

▲ **The Thames at Putney**
Oil
23 × 30.5 cm
(9 × 12 in)
This lively scene conjures up a sunny day on the river.

22

The Project
Ruin in a landscape with pen and wash

Paulette Fedarb

Paulette Fedarb offers various viewpoints to make the most of some romantic ruins in Leicestershire, painted in pen and wash

For this painting project, I looked for a subject that had atmosphere and interesting compositional opportunities. The 13th-century ruins of Grace Dieu Priory in Leicestershire seemed to be just what I wanted. I chose to work in pen and wash because I love the fluidity of this medium and the mixture of painting and drawing that is involved.

If you have not tried pen and wash before, I hope the project will inspire you to do so. Work freely – a few unintentional blobs here and there will not matter – but resist the temptation to use pencil first. That could incline you to merely ink over the lines, which can look insensitive. It takes courage at first, but try – it is worthwhile.

Use a large brush for the washes and not too fine a nib for the penwork, otherwise it may catch on the paper. A Not surface paper is suitable, providing reasonable tooth for the wash while being smooth enough for the pen. I used watercolour washes, but diluted ink washes could be an alternative for you. If you choose acrylic inks, make sure the brushes are rinsed immediately after use or they will harden.

▲ *A general view taken from a high vantage point.*

At this stage, perhaps I should confess my trepidation about encouraging you to work from someone else's photographs. I have always urged students to use sketchbooks and work from life in preference, or at least to take their own photographs. The question is one of direct experience. Every place has its own feel, which will influence an artist's response. In working from someone else's photograph this vital factor is missing and the resulting picture can appear lifeless.

◀ *Detail of the left-hand wall taken from ground level.*

◀ *Detail of the right-hand gable taken from ground level.*

By offering alternative viewpoints, I have tried to give a more comprehensive sense of location to help overcome this difficulty. Be inventive; alter and reposition shapes according to the picture you want to make. You will see how I have done this on the following pages.

This is a romantic subject. Colour and tone will be important, so give these careful thought. Consider the time of day as well – do not feel constrained by the light depicted. You might prefer a softer ambience, such as that occurring at dusk, or greater emphasis on form and texture, with stronger tonal contrast. There are many possibilities.

In describing this project I have refrained from giving precise instructions, preferring to leave decisions to you. It does not matter how simple or complex you make your picture. What does matter is that you should produce something essentially your own, even though your starting point was my photographs.

The Method

▶ *Detail of the left-hand wall from the first sketch.*

The ruins of Grace Dieu Priory are near where I live, which meant that as well as the photographs I had first-hand experience. Although it was January and bitterly cold, I was able to make a couple of sketches on the spot to provide information (*above and opposite*). I worked swiftly, starting with broad swathes of colour, using a 19 mm (¾ in) flat brush. Then, with a dip pen and black Indian ink, I drew on top, the ink and colour running together where the paper was still wet (shown in the foliage). More colour and ink drawing were added until I achieved what I needed, by which time the cold had got the better of me.

I then had the photographs and two sketches upon which to base my final picture. The time had come to make decisions. Two things came to the fore – composition and atmosphere, the latter of which would be directly related to colour and tone.

As it stands, the site is too spread out for a satisfactory pictorial composition, as can be

seen from the photograph on p. 104. This meant some condensing of the subject was necessary. I also needed to emphasize the verticals for a more interesting arrangement.

The upper photograph on p.105 shows how the foreshortened view of the wall alters the aspect of the ruins and gives the appearance of a tall, chimney-like shape. Although that photograph and the one below it, and their corresponding sketches, look like two separate units, they were the ends of a continuous middle section.

The two uprights, the 'chimney' and the right-hand gable, would form the dominant elements in the final picture. The large working sketch on p.108 shows how I integrated these two forms, although I was not happy with the dark arch in the centre. It was heavy and prevented the eye travelling back, with the result that everything appeared to be parallel to the picture plane. In other words, the picture went up and down and from side to side, but there was no sense of recession. I had felt from the beginning that atmosphere was a vital part of

this project, and it was lacking here. I am a romantic and any subject that has a spooky dimension catches my imagination.

Large brush

For the final version, I decided to work on a toned paper (grey Canson Mi-Teintes). Watercolours on toned papers create interesting, subdued effects and I frequently use them in preference to white papers.

I began in the same way as the sketches, brushing on washes of colour (Winsor Blue, Raw Umber and Olive Green). I always use a large brush at this stage in order to keep the work open and free. The perennial problem is to retain that initial freshness and not sacrifice it to over-working, which happens so easily in the desire to get enough content into a picture.

Learning from the experience of making my unsatisfactory third sketch, I cut the central arch in half and left out the dark tone. The substituted light area leads the viewer's eye on a diagonal line from the bottom right-hand corner, through the half

▲ *Detail of the gable.*

arch and towards the distant central tree, which provides a focal point. This movement is reinforced by the light wall of the gabled building on the right. Thus I achieved the recession that was previously lacking. The left side of the picture was treated in a similar way. I used the exaggerated fore-shortening of the second photograph, but left it more nebulous in order to add an element of mystery.

I tried to make much of the play between developed areas and those that are less defined. This brings movement and interest, equivalent to music with its loud and soft passages. It would be boring if a symphony were played at the same pitch all the way through. I make this point because less experienced painters often think that every inch of paper or canvas must be conscientiously worked or the picture will look unfinished. In the course of painting, one learns not what to put in but what to leave out.

Once the overall composition had been established with the initial colour washes, I began to crystallize the shapes with a pen, pulling out the textures and building up the character of the drawing, always mindful of the atmosphere I wanted to create. The picture progressed through several layers of colour and ink, which is typical of the way I work in this medium. I enjoy the constant switch between brush and pen. It both liberates and disciplines my ideas, and interrelates drawing and painting.

Emphasizing contrast

I brought in a few more colours: Cadmium Yellow to differentiate the planes of the walls; Indigo to intensify tone in the foliage; Payne's Grey for the sky. The sky is the only part that was carried out in a one-off action, using a round No. 10 brush. It has a spontaneous look set against the weighty, static appearance of the stones – again, that sense of contrast.

I find pen and wash a lovely medium, combining unique qualities of painting and drawing. I hope that in doing this project you have been able to share my enthusiasm for it

▼ *Paulette's working sketch, with an unsatisfactory central passage.*

and will now feel sufficiently stimulated to explore it further.

In my project, I have tried to show how you can use photography without becoming a slave to it. It has its practical uses, but should be used with discretion. Do not sacrifice your own creativity on its altar. Make your drawings and paintings from life, or imagination, whenever you can.

I conclude with a few words about pens. In general, I prefer to use a dip pen for the variety of line that can be achieved. However, there are certain practical disadvantages in that you need both ink and water (for cleaning the nib) in addition to the pen. Technical and sketching pens are useful, as they require no extras, but I have yet to come across any that match the dip pen for versatility. I have a cartridge sketching pen that I use for quick notes and sketches, but if I want to incorporate colour, or work in the studio, I always revert to a dip pen. Once you have tried one, I think you will understand what I mean.

▲ **Ruin in a Landscape**
Pen and wash
35.5 × 53.5 cm
(14 × 21 in)
Paulette's finished painting possesses the element of mystery that befits its subject.

23

The Project
Winter sunlight on the snow

Margaret Glass

Margaret Glass sets up a lesson in the use of pastel and demonstrates its particular suitability for depicting a snowy scene

The velvety texture of really soft pastel on glass paper lends itself very well to depicting snow as the way light is reflected by the tiny pastel particles is similar to the way it is affected by snow crystals. The difficulty, of course, is the logistics of painting in the depths of winter when cold can creep up on you after only a short time. Thank goodness for the camera. We can have the luxury of painting snow while we are tucked up in the warm and I feel that this advantage outweighs the problems associated with using photographs.

▲ *The photograph of winter sunlight at Rougham.*

▶ *The preliminary sketch with the problem areas marked.*

When a friend showed me some snowy photographs he had taken I felt he had captured the sort of winter day when the sunlight is brilliant and the light clear. The mantle of snow, so clean and powdery, gave a silence and tranquillity – the sort of beauty that makes one feel good to be alive. I chose the photograph reproduced here (*left*) as the elements of that kind of day are all present. The only problem is that it does not work completely well as a composition for a painting. This is where we can come into our own as painters and overrule nature, uproot trees and buildings and place them in a more balanced and pleasing position.

The real point
Before being over-enthusiastic about such power, it is vital to analyse what is lacking in the composition so that what is needed can be assessed. Study the photograph and see if you can discern what is slightly uncomfortable about the picture as a whole. The elements that I was excited about were, most importantly, the sunlit end of the hedge in the foreground and the shadows crossing the path. Then there was the juxtaposition of the dark shadows and light in the hedge on the right, and thirdly, the sun lighting the church tower with that one lovely shadow giving the aerial perspective to the church in a stroke.

I decided to enhance all these elements in the painting and keep them in the forefront of my thinking, as they would transmit the beauty of the scene. It is all too easy to get carried away with technique, but that is subservient to the real point of painting this subject – to communicate my response to such a day and to say to the viewer: 'Look at the sunlight; look how it lights up the snow; look at the rich shadows cast. Isn't it glorious?'

Obviously, the practicality of the painting process still had to be addressed. I have drawn a quick sketch to highlight the areas where I perceived problems (*left*). Look at the sketch to decide what you feel the problems might be and tackle them in your own composition.

The Method

In the pencil sketch shown opposite I have numbered what I regard as the problem areas of the composition:

1 The church tower is too far to the right of the picture.

2 The eye is not sure whether to travel to the end of the hedge in the right foreground or to the left and out of the picture. This is called unresolved duality and makes for an uncomfortable composition.

3 The height of the background trees, especially the central area, takes attention from the tower.

Now look at my second sketch (*below*). That is the composition I was happy with, so I roughly worked it out on to the glass paper, using the darks to place the composition.

As an aid to showing aerial perspective, the use of warm colours to come forward and cool colours to retreat is vital and I was aware of this from the first stage of the painting (*above*). Notice the cool green-greys in the distance and the warm blue-grey in the shadows of the pathway.

At this stage I used the side of the pastel to put in the sky area with a very pale, cool blue

to fill the tooth of the paper quickly. A lot more pastel had to be layered over the surface to achieve a smooth, though not flat, sky. Layers of cool Lemon Yellow placed on the tree line and a mixture of warm and cool blues created a sky with depth.

I placed the dark tones in the bushes more firmly, using both a dark, cool blue-grey and dark warm brown. The darkest dark in the hedge on the right, below the church tower, is a very dark, cool green-grey. This could be

▲ *The judicious use of cool and warm colours gives the effect of aerial perspective.*

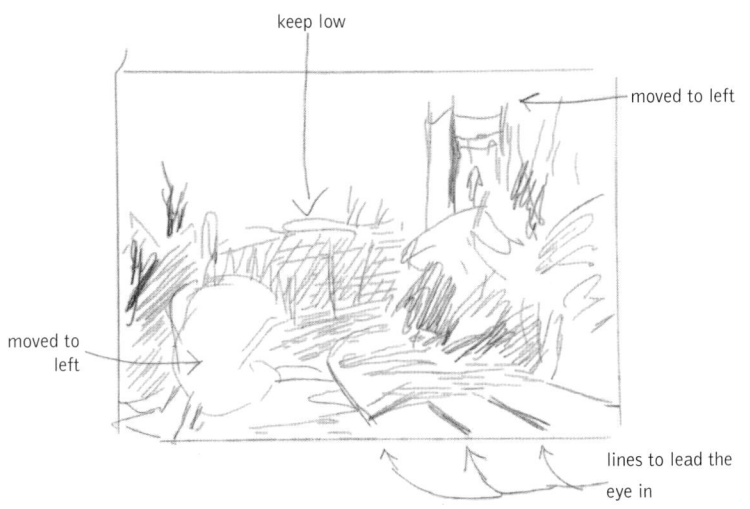

keep low

moved to left

moved to left

lines to lead the eye in

◀ *Margaret's second sketch shows how she solved the compositional problems.*

mistaken for black, but is not as harsh. I find the Sennelier range of darks excellent, staying as soft as the lighter tints.

The tower has been very loosely indicated and that lovely shadow giving the almost three-dimensional effect is a warm blue grey. Other than a few touches of detail I left it as finished. It is pleasing when a few strokes achieve all that is required. The skill sometimes is to know when to leave well alone. On the extreme right I just touched one or two places with the same Lemon Yellow used in the sky. This was to check that the middle tones, which are chosen in relationship to the darks, were dark enough and that the light tones would sing out.

Impasto effect

Next I worked on the background trees to the left of the church and moved forward to the hedge in front (*above*). Within the layers of cool blue-green is a warmer green-grey and touches of warm French Ultramarine. On the left, where the sun is catching a small area, warm yellow ochres, pale Cadmium Red and French Ultramarine were used. The areas behind the hedge had to be cool to enable the warm colours to come forward and sing.

At this stage it was tempting to finish the pathway, but I wanted that to be really fresh and inviting, so I moved on to the hedge below and to the right of the church tower. I did not go straight from the background trees to this area before tackling the warm sunlit hedge in the foreground as I wanted the detail and highlights on the right-hand edge to be more muted so I could constantly refer to, and not take away from, that lovely sunny area.

Although there are detailed highlights on the church tower, I wanted the hedge beneath to be fairly loose. Too much detail all through a painting can make it very busy and not restful on the eye. In this area I was trying to achieve form and colour only. The most detail was in the foreground hedge, the highlights at the base of the background trees, where the path bends round the corner, and the church tower. This helps the eye to travel through the picture. The challenge was to simplify, but keep the form and shape. The juxtaposition of warm and cool tints helped enormously with this.

Finally, the pathway was defined with very loose strokes of cool blue-grey, Coeruleum and French Ultramarine. Lemon Yellow, very pale Raw Sienna, Cadmium Red and French Ultramarine were used for the sunny highlights. Nowhere in the painting did I use white, as it is too high key and harsh.

The painting was photographed with the light coming from the left-hand side. This shows up what looks like an impasto effect. It was achieved by compressing the pastel firmly on to the surface so that it would not fall off, even if the painting were knocked.

Looking at the finished painting, I can almost hear the crunch of the snow underfoot – and if I have achieved that for others my work was well worth while.

▲ **Winter Sunlight, Rougham**
Pastel on glass paper
30.5 × 40.5 cm
(12 × 16 in)
Cool and warm colours and the use of pastel have resulted in a painting that speaks unmistakably of a crisp, snowy day.

24

The Project
Picture design with hollyhocks

Ann Blockley

Ann Blockley draws inspiration and reference from some photographs, but goes on to paint pictures of a more romantic flavour

The idea of working from photographs is abhorrent to many painters. It is despised as a type of cheating to which no serious artist would stoop. I think the important issue is the way in which the photograph is used. To paint a facsimile of a photographed image does seem a waste of time, but it is a different proposition to use photographs as reference material or in conjunction with sketches.

The trouble with snapshots is that they are often flawed. The colours or tonal values are often distorted or the composition and background may be boring or unsuitable. The painter, however, can play at being a magician by juggling images on paper, piecing bits of photographs together like a jigsaw. You can add, subtract, enhance and strengthen; play with the colours, tones and composition. You use your artist's licence to build up an illustration, just as you would if you were painting on the spot. In other words, the photograph is merely a useful reminder and starting point for creative work. Few people can rely solely on imagination to conjure up painting ideas and it is not always convenient or viable to paint or draw from life.

Painting flowers brings practical problems. Not everyone has access to gardens or fields. In a vase indoors, flowers have the irritating habit of blossoming, wilting or gliding sneakily out of position. Obviously, painting from life is rewarding, but the back-up of a photograph can be reassuring. This project uses photographs of flowers as reference for creating one or more paintings.

The decisions

These hollyhocks were growing in riotous profusion in a cottage garden. There was every shade from darkest maroon to the palest shell pink. They mingled in romantic chaos. How could I select one design from the endless possibilities displayed? I took several photographs and chose the three shown here as starting points for two different paintings.

Do not simply follow what I have done – deciding which elements to use, combine or reject is where the fun begins. You could select a small detail for an intimate painting or include all the flowers for a more panoramic view. You have to decide on the shape and size of the painting – whether to add height or width. Will the picture have lots of contrast in terms of colour and tone or be subtle and delicate?

The picture could be quite graphic – for example, a single spike on a simple background – or be very busy, even pretty. You could paint in great detail or very loosely.

▲ *Photograph 1.*

▲ *Photograph 2.*

▲ *Photograph 3.*

There is an infinite number of possibilities. Each of us tackling this project should finish with a different picture that is an expression of our own response to the subject.

The first photograph (*left*) is of dreamy pink saucers of colour in front of some cottage windows. The second (*above*) is also by the cottage, with full red flowers dark against the pale windows. Both of these are interesting flower groups with plenty of detail. Each is an interesting composition in its own right, divided by the dark wall below and paler window above. I have to decide whether they look uncomfortable with their buds chopped off the top. How much shall I let these sorts of photographic facts influence my painting decisions?

The third photograph (*above right*) shows the hollyhocks in a more natural setting. It includes all the tops of the flowers, but the composition is unbalanced and boring. The central stalk is rather bare. Perhaps I could change the shape and colours or combine it with something else to make this more interesting?

Our project is to create one or two pieces from these three photographs. You do not have to use all of them, or you may use bits from all three. You might take only sections or make slight alterations. On the other hand, you could change the whole concept to create something new.

I work in watercolour, but as I would like this project to be more about thinking, ideas and planning than about techniques, you can use any medium you feel comfortable with.

The Method

▼ **Cottage Garden Hollyhocks**
Watercolour
76 × 56 cm
(30 × 22 in)
Here the hollyhocks are transposed to a luxuriant garden setting.

For my first painting I considered photographs 1 and 2 as reference material. The first is an informative photograph with its clear close-up of flowers and leaves. The tops of the stalks would need to be completed where the camera had pruned them. This would make a vertical painting to echo the shape of the flowers. The background could be altered by eliminating the window, as I decided that the vertical frames are distracting. All this would help to make a pleasant enough picture, but too straightforward for someone who likes to show off!

Another idea would be to make similar alterations to the second photograph, which has a corresponding layout, and piece the two pictures together. This would make a squarish or horizontal shape, however, and for me it is virtually compulsory for hollyhocks to be portrayed in a portrait format.

I wanted to use the information in the photographs to remind me how hollyhocks grow and the formation of the flowers, but I decided to radically change the layout and mood in my painting. I thought back to the cottage garden where I took these photographs. It was a rampant, luxurious mass of flowers and I decided to re-create an impression of the whole scene. This was somewhere I visited and it was important to capture a memory rather than just reproduce paintings of individual snapshots. Snatched separately, these flower portraits are pretty, but only fragments taken from a whole experience. I wanted to combine the elements to make a personal painting.

Altered colours

You can look at the finished picture to piece together the bits I have added, altered or left out. The pale pink flowers on the left of the first photograph appear at the middle bottom of the painting, while the pink flowers on the right of the photograph have changed places and been blurred. I did not want all the flowers to be equally defined, as some needed to stand forward for attention and others to recede.

The dark maroon flowers in the second photograph had a rather sharp, acidic tinge that clashed with the romantic softness of the pink hollyhocks. I used the photographs to assist with the general layout of the flora, but altered the colours to a paler peach hue, losing certain petals into the background with drifts of colours in order to add depth. I completed the tops of the stems that had worried me. The spindly knobbles protruding from the chunky flower forms are vital parts of the hollyhocks' character and I had to include them.

I changed the tonal patterns in all the flowers described so far. They had been photographed against the reflected light on cottage windows. The window panes were irrelevant to me, so I placed the flowers in a more leafy, verdant setting – pale on a dark background. The hollyhock leaves were treated quite simply, with loose, pale shapes not clearly described. The reference material shows them in clear detail, but if I used all the information on offer I would end up with a painted photograph. The red flowers on the left of the painting are an invention and they are pictured against the light. If the background were dark all over, it would be too heavy for the airy cottage-garden romance I intended to stage.

I added some leaves around the edges of this pale area, like a halo around the flowers. Without these, the painting seemed to slip away into the corner and I wanted to anchor attention on the flowers. I used a fairly limited palette because it is a busy composition with plenty of tonal variation and too many colours would be distracting.

I would never rely on the colours shown in a photograph for information. The colours printed in this book will vary from those in the snapshot and the colours of the latter are dictated at the photographic laboratory. By the time it is my turn to translate them into watercolour, the true colours of the garden could be totally lost.

To solve this, I often jot down colour notes when I see my subjects – either mentally or in a notebook. Not vague observations like 'blue/green leaves', which would be open to later interpretation, but notes such as 'leaves – Monestial Blue with Cadmium Yellow.' I can use this information at a future date in the knowledge that, even if not entirely accurate, it will conjure up something of the atmosphere I experienced at the time.

Different sizes

My second painting is based on the third photograph. It has a lot in common with the first picture in terms of colour, tonal patterns and format. It is interesting to see how two pictures can share characteristics, but still be subtly different.

You cannot appreciate it here, but the impact of each painting varies considerably as a result of their different sizes. The first painting covers a panoramic A2 sheet of watercolour paper, whereas the second is no bigger than this page – a much richer, more concentrated image.

It would be fascinating to see everyone's pictures together, just like a garden that is overflowing with hollyhocks, each with its own personality. I hope that this project has given you food for thought. It is good to paint from life whenever you are able, but enjoy using your own snapshots if that is all that is available.

Try not to allow photographs to make you lazy. Your camera is just a tool and you must make it work for you in as creative a way as possible.

▲ **Hollyhocks**
Watercolour
30.5 × 20.5 cm
(12 × 8 in)
In this painting you can see the floral elements Ann has used from the third photograph, with extra petals and stems added here and there. She has chopped out much of the solid leafy background to create a more interesting and lively pattern of light and dark graphic shapes. The tonal values of the picture have been practically reversed.

25

Composition
with snow

David Curtis

David Curtis
shows how to
paint a snow
scene in oils.
Note how he
analyses his
subject and decide
upon your own
composition

Snow gives a simplifying dimension to the landscape, breaking up the uniformity of shapes and offering a chance to explore subtle shadows against a lit, white surface.

While it is possible, though not always comfortable, to work outdoors in these conditions, there is often some justification in working from photographic reference. At such times there may be much more subject matter available than can possibly be put on canvas on each outing.

Three slight variations of a strongly lit, well-composed snow subject are illustrated here. My rough oil layout (*right*) is mainly based on the first view but also takes the best of the elements from the others. You can choose to paint any of the views or blend them together as I have done.

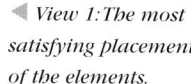

◀ *View 1: The most satisfying placement of the elements.*

▲ *View 3: A bolder composition.*

◀ *View 2: More buildings are visible.*

The Method

I felt that the first view offers the most satisfying placement of the elements in the scene. A little more of the outhouse on the far right is included in my sketch to make more sense of the shape, and there is a hint of the backdrop continuity. I decided to substitute the older-style cottage with the snow-laden roof from the third view for the modern dormer house. This was not only personal

choice as to architectural styles; I considered that this shape punctuates the backdrop more effectively. I think this works and I hope has the feel of immediacy, as if it were produced on site. I would make such alterations to any subject as a matter of course if I thought it necessary.

There is something quite satisfying visually about the blue shadow forms across the snowy road in the first view. They seem to draw the eye towards the lit face of the main cottage most effectively.

Apart from the adjustments I made to the composition here and there, I also lifted the key slightly to give a more airy quality to the painting.

In this scene there is a lot of tonal contrast, strong colour values and a good composition. Above all, it is a great drawing exercise with some lovely perspective lines. If you are a little doubtful about your drawing skills at this stage, try some thumbnail sketches to get

▲ *David's rough oil layout.*

▶ *An intermediate stage, with broad masses of colour.*

the proportions right and to ensure everything is placed pleasingly on the board or canvas, then forge ahead. Keep the brushwork loose and free, and take care that you do not feel too constrained by the photographic image. It is easy to become bogged down in a slavish representation of the photographic image, and too many paintings on exhibition walls bear witness to the artist having made that mistake.

The charm of the subject and its initial appeal was the simplicity of the broad shapes, form and colour. The artist rarely knows at the outset if it is possible to retain, through the medium of paint, that discipline of a simple approach as the work progresses. The key lies in developing the technique to be able to transmit the language of the shape effectively without saying too much. If one sweeping brushstroke, correctly mixed and vigorously applied, more or less makes a convincing statement, leave it said and

do not be tempted to feather the edges to try to get it more exact. Overworking will almost always kill the spontaneity of the image and the result will have a tight, lifeless feel.

Establishing the composition

I started with a toned board and sketched in the main forms. I then stated the extremes of light by rubbing out, right back to the white board surface, those areas representing sunlit snow surfaces.

Next I placed one or two strong darks to set the basic tonal scene and proceeded from there with a series of broad areas. I related and matched one to the other, so constructing the feeling of the old cottage and its outbuilding in the foreground (see the intermediate stage on p.119).

I tried to make a little more of the shape of the conifer flanking the cottage on the right than is suggested from the photograph.

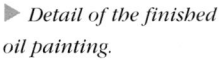

▶ *Detail of the finished oil painting.*

Although such trees are not my favourites for inclusion in a painting, this one serves as a useful dark mass in an ideal position.

Working around the painting on this basis, I continued to block in the snow and the bluey shadows in the road surface, being aware of the need to keep an eye on the relative tonal value of this surface to all the other areas of the painting. To gain a real feeling of light on the ground, I felt it would be necessary to pitch the sky area well down in key. I placed the sky after massing in the background forms, all of which punch the buildings forward as well as lending a feeling of space and a three-dimensional quality.

Adding some figures

By now the entire board had been covered with broad areas of paint and it was a question of searching out the little nuances and subtleties that add interest and emphasis to the composition.

I worked on the feathered feel of the bushes in the foreground against the snow and the furrows and ruts in the roadway, which gave scope for more localized blue shadow forms. These were adjusted as need be from the reality of the photograph in order to make a pleasing balance of tone and form.

For a feeling of life and scale, I also included one or two figures. If you are inhibited about placing figures for fear of spoiling the piece, put them in the middle distance where they will not loom large. They can be only loosely described, as in my painting, but will still be quite convincing.

You can see my finished attempt on this page and I hope that it will be of help in your own endeavours.

▲ **Late Snow, Harwell**
Oil
25.5 × 35.5 cm
(10 × 14 in)
A strong composition and cool colours make this a convincing scene of a village under snow.

David Easton
works in both watercolour and pastel, showing how a simple grouping can be lit in different ways to provide a change of emphasis

This is an open-ended project involving a motif composed of natural vegetable forms. Assemble a few items obtained from your greengrocer or supermarket and set them up as I describe. Choose vegetables that appeal to you for their shape, colour, texture and intrinsic tone – some light, some dark, some striped. If you tackle this project in the autumn you will be spoilt for choice with the varieties of gourd that are available, some with cracked, gnarled and encrusted rinds, others with glowing, gaudy colours and zany striped patterns.

▼ *A small charcoal sketch, quickly setting down a full range of tones, from the white paper to rich black charcoal.*

Arrange your group of, say, five to nine items on a board or tray – odd numbers make a better grouping than even numbers. Use a light paper or fabric base in order to get clear cast shadows and reflections into the objects. The board can be set in a good light, either natural or artificial, in a low position. You should be able to turn the board or move around it, so that sidelit views and views lit from behind (known as *contre-jour*) are available.

Using charcoal or soft pencils, make some studies that explore the light and shade on and around the vegetables. Other sketches can focus on the colour composition and

some linear drawings might investigate the rhythms in the group. Make your studies from at least a couple of viewpoints, exploring both side and back lighting.

Use both wet and dry media in your preliminary studies of your vegetable group. I have not specified just one medium for your finished piece; in this project the value is as much in the making of studies as in producing a completed painting. However, I have shown both watercolour and a pastel and I suggest that you choose one of these for your painting. My illustrations show how each medium can help to focus attention on specific qualities in the group.

◄ Charcoal and pastel on a khaki-grey paper that gives a richer range of middle tones and makes the artist put in the light rather than reserve it.

◄ A watercolour study exploring the colour composition. The cool shadow colours were laid in first.

The Method

My watercolour painting (*below*) is a simple distribution of the objects in a landscape format. I have given close attention to the shapes of the gourds, placing them to give a varied groundline and skyline, with the cast shadows linking the composition. These shadows are rendered in colours that complement the yellows of the gourds. The warm tinted paper helps to harmonize the piece. Had I been working on a white paper I would have made more of the setting, creating some tone changes at the top. In this instance, the precise amount of space above and below the objects is critical when it comes to the placing of a mount.

As with the watercolour study on the previous page, I began with cold colours and glazed the yellows over, working wet-over-dry throughout. My watercolour palette for the two sketches comprised Lemon Yellow, Yellow Ochre, Cadmium Yellow, Alizarin Crimson, Cadmium Red, Light Red, Prussian Blue, Coeruleum, French Ultramarine and Winsor Violet.

The pastel (*opposite*), where backlighting has been used, is more of a tonal work. Most of the surfaces of objects are in shadow. The grey pastel paper can be seen showing through in places, especially at the centre top. Starting with charcoal, I built in the traditional way from darks through middle tones to the lights. Finger blending was used on the objects and in the cast shadows. Hatched strokes in the rest of the setting provide textural contrast. As in the watercolour, I have grouped together the richer coloured and patterned gourds in order to provide a focal area.

As the work progressed, I sought to play off sharp contrasts between objects and the close-toned transitions, reflecting the many subtly different tonal relationships

▶ **Gourds**
Watercolour on tinted Bockingford paper
25.5 × 35.5 cm
(10 × 14 in)
A simple composition that derives much of its interest from the balance of colour.

between objects and shadows. I often work to a square format, finding it challenging, satisfying and a refreshing change from the ubiquitous 2:3 proportion.

It may not be immediately obvious, but both the pastel and the watercolour were made from the same grouping of gourds. They were viewed from positions about 90 degrees apart. The *contre-jour* pastel and the sidelit watercolour clearly illustrate the capacity of light to transform a motif.

You will have seen from my list that my watercolour choice is a light palette of mainly primary and secondary colours. When working with pastels I find that a good number of tertiaries is invaluable. It is possible to mix pastels to a degree, both physically and visually, but not so effectively on a small scale. I need to have about 50 colours in the box.

I hope that you will see other applications for this project, perhaps choosing a set of objects that have a particular appeal to you. I have enjoyed doing similar things with sea flotsam and shells, for example. It is good to have a break from man-made objects with all their ellipses.

▲ **Gourds**
Pastel on grey paper
30.5 × 30.5 cm
(12 × 12 in)
A backlit view results in a painting where tonal values take precedence over colour.

About the Artists

Norman Battershill RBA, ROI, PS paints in all media and is particularly known for his atmospheric landscapes. For many years he has been a regular contributor of instructional articles to *Leisure Painter*. In 1987 he received the Royal Institute of Oil Painters Stanley Grimm Award and in 1999 the ROI Cornelissen prize. Author of more than a dozen art instruction books, Norman Battershill writes and paints from his home in rural north Dorset.

David Bellamy specializes mainly in painting mountain and wild coastal scenes. He has written and illustrated nine books, several of which are published by HarperCollins, made four films on watercolour painting and runs watercolour courses in the UK and overseas. Through painting and writing he endeavours to bring about a greater awareness of threats to the natural environment. He is a patron of the Marine Conservation Society's Seas for Life Appeal. David has been featured on radio and television in numerous programmes, including his television series *Painting Wild Wales*.

Linda Birch MSIAD studied fine art and graphic design at Folkestone School of Art in Kent. She paints in oil, watercolour and pastel and has exhibited with the Royal Watercolour Society, as well as holding solo shows throughout the UK. She is an elected member of the Society of Industrial Artists and Designers. Linda is the author of several art instruction books, including *You Can Paint Oils*, published by HarperCollins. She has also illustrated over 200 children's books, in addition to illustrations for the BBC children's programmes *Bagpuss*, *The Clangers* and *Jackanory*. Linda teaches classes in County Durham and at Higham Hall in Cumbria and also demonstrates her techniques nationally.

Ann Blockley moved to the Cotswolds in 1975 when her father, the painter G. John Blockley, opened a gallery there. She studied at Gloucestershire College of Art and Design and at Brighton Polytechnic before commencing a successful career as a freelance illustrator. Commissions have included images for educational and reference books, tapestry designs, greetings cards, giftware and packaging for such companies as Marks & Spencer, Laura Ashley and Ehrman. She is the author of several books published by HarperCollins, has made a video and runs flower painting workshops from early spring to late autumn.

Aggy Boshoff was born in The Hague, the Netherlands. She graduated with an MA in Law and practised as an advocate in Amsterdam from 1976 to 1986. After a period of study at the Rietveld Art Academy in Amsterdam, she trained at St Martin's School of Art and the Heatherley School of Art in London. She has exhibited her work extensively in the UK as well as in the Netherlands and Hong Kong.

Ray Campbell Smith FRSA is a prolific and versatile painter, specializing in watercolours. His work is represented in many collections in the UK and abroad and he has held more than 41 solo shows in the many galleries that regularly exhibit his work, both in this country and abroad. He has made 12 highly successful instructional videos on watercolour and has written ten books on painting, including several major bestsellers.

Alwyn Crawshaw SEA, BWS, PNAPA, PSAA UA (Hon.), FRSA works in watercolour, oil and acrylic. He is a Fellow of the Royal Society of Arts, a member of the Society of Equestrian Artists and the British Watercolour Society, president of the National Acrylic Painters Association, founder of the Society of Amateur Artists, and an honorary member of the United Society of Artists. He has written 24 books for HarperCollins, including *The Artist at Work* – his autobiography. Alwyn has made eight television series (66 half-hour programmes). He is listed in the current edition of *Who's Who in Art* and the Marquis *Who's Who in the World*.

Harley Crossley paints exclusively in oils using knives, and is the acknowledged expert in the UK in this technique. His large maritime works are much sought after by collectors around the world, and a series of these paintings grace one of the stairways on the prestigious cruise ship *Queen Elizabeth 2*. Several of his paintings have been reproduced as fine art prints and he has made a series of teaching videos. Harley now divides his time between painting in his studio and demonstrating and lecturing on cruise ships around the world.

David Curtis ROI, RSMA headed an engineering design team until 1988 when he became a full-time painter. Essentially a *plein air* and figurative painter, working in both oil and watercolour, he won the first prize in the Singer & Friedlander/*Sunday Times* Watercolour Competition in 1992 and the second prize in 1997. David is the author of several books and videos, and his work is held in private collections both nationally and abroad. David joined the selection committee for the Singer & Friedlander/*Sunday Times* Watercolour Competition in 1998.

David Easton RI lives and works in Leicester. His working life has encompassed graphic design and periods of teaching in schools and colleges, notably in the sphere of Adult Education. He continues to visit many art clubs and societies to offer critical appraisals, and he tutors painting courses in the UK and France. David's published works include books on watercolour painting as well as numerous magazine articles. He exhibits in galleries throughout the UK.

Michael B. Edwards followed a successful career in engineering and business before becoming a full-time painter 12 years ago. His art training was at night school at colleges such as Manchester and Hammersmith. Michael paints in oil, watercolour and acrylic and his work is included in major galleries in the UK and in the galleries of the Royal Society of Marine Artists and other professional societies in London. He has held solo shows annually for the past seven years. Michael has had three books published and writes regularly for painting magazines.

Paulette Fedarb trained at Chelsea School of Art and Hornsey College of Art. For many years she taught painting while continuing to build her portfolio. In 1987 she gave up teaching to concentrate on her own work. She is the author of several magazine articles as well as two books on the technique of pen and wash. Her work has appeared in many solo and mixed shows, and is held in both public and private collections. She is a member of the National Society of Painters, Sculptors and Printmakers.

James Fletcher-Watson RI, RBA specializes in painting landscapes in watercolour. He has held one-man exhibitions in America, Australia and London and holds an annual exhibition at his own gallery at Windrush, Gloucestershire. James has also exhibited at the Royal Academy, London and has received an award at the Paris Salon. He has written five teaching books on watercolour painting and three videos have been made showing him painting out of doors.

Stanford Gibbons received a formal training in graphics and fine art at the Ryland Memorial School of Art. He began work as a graphic artist in advertising agencies, progressing into advertising management and marketing before forming his own publicity company. He founded Cader Idris Painting Holidays, a hotel in Snowdonia that specialized in painting holidays, at which he was principal tutor. He now combines concentrating upon his own art at his home in Sussex with tutoring painting holidays abroad.

Margaret Glass PS, FRSA, MP, SPF is recognized as one of today's leading pastellists. She is past vice-president of the *Société des Artistes des Pastellistes Français* and a member of the English Pastel Society. In 1992 she was awarded the title 'Maitre Pastellist' by the *Société des Artistes Français*, only the 11th artist to receive this distinction. More recently she has also built up a growing reputation as an oil painter. Published works include magazine articles, plus a book on pastel painting. Margaret has exhibited in France

and New York as well as the UK, and runs painting courses in pastel.

Moira Grice studied art and graphics at Harrow and Newcastle Art Colleges and later gained a BA (Hons) degree in Education at Portsmouth University. Following a successful career in advertising, publishing and as a freelance designer and illustrator, she has taught art in Further Education for the past 20 years. She demonstrates her drawing and painting methods to art societies along the south coast of England and exhibits her oil, watercolour and pastel paintings in London, East Anglia and West Sussex.

Lesley Hollands studied fine art at the West Surrey and Brighton Colleges of Art and Design. She is a practising artist whose work has been shown and sold at the Mall, Bankside, Westminster and Wykham Galleries. She has had work accepted for the Singer & Friedlander/ *Sunday Times* Watercolour Exhibition on several occasions and has work in private collections in Paris, London, Australia, New Zealand and the USA. Lesley teaches at West Dean College in West Sussex and Highfield School, Liphook.

Wendy Jelbert SWA, NAPA was born in Sussex and for many years was Deputy Head of Further Education at Wyvern School, Southampton. She has exhibited extensively in London and throughout England. Her published works include several books on painting in watercolour, line and wash, acrylic and water-soluble pencils. *You Can Paint Mixed Media* is due to be published by HarperCollins in 2002. Wendy is a demonstrator for many leading art materials companies.

Ronald Jesty RBA worked for many years as a freelance graphic designer. His painting subjects – usually of still lifes and the land- and seascapes of Somerset and Dorset – are almost always in his preferred medium of watercolour. Elected a member of the RBA in 1982, he has also exhibited at many other venues such as the Royal Watercolour Society, the Royal West of England Academy, the Royal Academy, and the Singer and Friedlander/*Sunday Times* Watercolour Competition. Ronald has written and contributed to many books and magazines on drawing and painting.

John McCombs NDD, ROI, RBA, FRSA, MAFA studied painting at St Martin's School of Art in London between 1962 and 1967. In 1966 he won

the College Prize and was awarded the David Murray Scholarship by the Royal Academy. Listed in *Who's Who in Art*, he exhibits mostly in London and Manchester and at his own studio and the John McCombs Gallery in Delph, Lancashire.

Christine McKechnie was born in 1943. She trained at Southampton and Kingston Schools of Art in the early 1960s. She started making her collages in 1968 and uses exclusively hand-painted paper, cut, applied and layered, employing many hundreds of pieces. In 1983 she won a special award for her work at the Royal Academy. She has had numerous London solo exhibitions and her pictures feature in a number of private and public collections.

Ronald Morgan RBA, ROI works in oil, watercolour and drawing media. He has exhibited at the Royal Academy, the Royal Society of British Artists, the Royal Institute of Oil Painters, the Royal Institute of Painters in Water Colours, the New English Art Club and the Royal Society of Marine Artists, as well as at the Paris Salon and most provincial British galleries. He has won many art awards and has work in private collections worldwide.

Alan Oliver was born in 1937 and trained originally as an engineer and commercial designer. For a number of years he ran his own studio specializing in technical animated-film production, but in 1983 he decided to close his commercial practice to concentrate on his painting. Since then he has exhibited with the Royal Institute of Painters in Water Colours, the Royal Institute of Oil Painters, the Pastel Society, the Royal Watercolour Society and the Royal Academy. He has had three books published about his work and writes regularly for art magazines, both nationally and internationally.

John Patchett attended Grimsby School of Art, Kingston-upon-Thames College of Art and Brighton College of Art. He settled in Australia for 19 years before returning to England in 1994. Besides holding 30 successful solo shows in Australia and England, John has exhibited his pastels in Japan and New Zealand and with the Pastel Society, the Royal Society of Marine Artists and the Laing Exhibition at the Mall Galleries, London, where he was awarded the 'Guest's Choice' prize in 1997.

Index